W14 Productions in association with Neil McPherson
for the Finborough Theatre presents

The World Premiere

JAM
by Matt Parvin

FINBOROUGH | THEATRE
First performance at the Finborough Theatre: Tuesday, 23 May 2017.

JAM

by Matt Parvin

Cast in order of speaking

Bella	**Jasmine Hyde**
Kane	**Harry Melling**

The action takes place over one evening in a school in a rural town.

The performance lasts approximately ninety minutes.

There will be no interval.

Director	**Tommo Fowler**
Designer	**Emma Bailey**
Lighting Designer	**Peter Harrison**
Sound Designer and Composer	**Alexandra Faye Braithwaite**
Movement and Fight Director	**Ailin Conant**
Production Manager	**Anoushka Hughes-Lewis**
Stage Manager	**Rachel Graham**
Producer	**Annabel Williamson**
Photography	**Mathew Foster**

Our patrons are respectfully reminded that, in this intimate theatre, any noise such as rustling programmes, talking or the ringing of mobile phones may distract the actors and your fellow audience-members.

We regret there is no admittance or re-admittance to the auditorium whilst the performance is in progress.

Jasmine Hyde | Bella

Trained at The Royal Academy of Dramatic Art.

Theatre includes *Not Moses* (Arts Theatre), *Pericles* (Royal Shakespeare Company), *The Coast of Utopia* (National Theatre), *Whose Life is it Anyway?* and *The Dog* (Frinton Summer Theatre), *Statements After An Arrest Under the Immorality Act* (Jermyn Street Theatre), *Death of a Cyclist* (Arcola Theatre), *Muswell Hill* (Orange Tree Theatre, Richmond), *A Midsummer Night's Dream* (Shakespeare's Globe), *Somniloquy* and *Why Can't We Live Together?* (Theatre503), *'06/'07/'05* and *Gaugleprixtown* (Menagerie Theatre Company), *The Rivals* (Theatre Royal Bath), *Gifts of War* and *Two Into War* (National Tour), *Charley's Aunt* (Northcott Theatre, Exeter), *Singer* (Oxford Stage Company), *Waters of the Moon* (Salisbury Playhouse) and *Tiny Dynamite* (Paines Plough and Frantic Assembly).

Film includes *The Unseen*, *The Truth Commissioner*, *Sins of a Father*, *A Distant Mirage*, *Runt*, *Other*, *Undo* and *Restoration*.

Television includes *Doctors*, *Holby City* and *Casualty*.

Radio includes many Radio 4 afternoon plays, *Book at Bedtime*, *Book of the Week* and *Poetry Please*.

Jasmine also plays Leonie Snell in *The Archers*.

Harry Melling | Kane

Trained at the London Academy of Music and Dramatic Art.

Theatre includes *King Lear* (The Old Vic), *Hand to God* (Vaudeville Theatre), *The Angry Brigade* (Bush Theatre and Paines Plough), *Peddling* (HighTide Festival Theatre, Arcola Theatre, and 59E59 Theaters, New York City), *King Lear* (Chichester Festival Theatre), *The Hothouse* and *When Did You Last See My Mother* (Trafalgar Studios), *Smack Family Robinson* (Rose Theatre, Kingston), *I Am A Camera* (Southwark Playhouse), *The School for Scandal* (Barbican Theatre) and *Women Beware Women* and *Mother Courage and Her Children* (National Theatre).

Television includes *Musketeers*, *Joe Mistry*, *Garrow's Law*, *Merlin*, *Just William and Friends* and *Crocodiles*.

Film includes *The Current War*, *Lost City of Z*, *Harry Potter and the Deathly Hallows*, *Harry Potter and the Order of the Phoenix*, *Harry Potter and the Prisoner of Azkaban*, *Harry Potter and the Chamber of Secrets*, *Harry Potter and the Philosopher's Stone*, *The Winds of Change*, *I Think Therefore* and *Felicity*.

Matt Parvin | Playwright

Matt Parvin is a playwright from Dorset. His professional debut *Two Roads* premiered at VAULT Festival in 2015, and he has adapted *Alice in Wonderland* (Edinburgh Festival and National Tour). His short plays include *Monster Party* and *You Maverick* (Arcola Theatre), *Everyday Horse* (Theatre503), *Roost,* winner of Best Script Prize (Oxford New Writing Festival) and *Somewhere Else Entirely* (Nuffield Theatre, Southampton). He has been a part of the Royal Court Young Writers Programme, the Arcola Theatre Writers Programme, and the Writers Collective at the Orange Tree Theatre, Richmond.

Tommo Fowler | Director

Productions at the Finborough Theatre include *Obama-ology* and *I Wish To Die Singing* (Winner of Studio Theatre Award for Best New Play), and as Resident Assistant Director, *Harajuku Girls* and *Sommer 14: A Dance of Death*.

Theatre includes the forthcoming production of *Mumburger* (Old Red Lion Theatre), *Griff Rhys Jones: Jones and Smith* (UK Tour), *Mumburger*, nominated for OffWestEnd Award for Best Female Performance (Archivist's Gallery), *Somewhere Else Entirely* (Nuffield Theatre, Southampton), *PLAY #13* (VAULT Festival), *Monster Party* (Arcola Theatre) and *The (Accidental) Death of Alan Bishop* (Pleasance London).

Assistant Direction includes *Passin' Thru* (Lyric Theatre, Hammersmith), *A Lovely Sunday for Creve Coeur* (Print Room) and *Rainbow*, winner of a Fringe First Award (Edinburgh Festival).

Emma Bailey | Designer

Productions at the Finborough Theatre includes *Bitches*.

Trained on the Motley Theatre Design Course, and was winner of the Linbury Prize for Stage and Design 2011.

Theatre includes *Double Double Act* (Unicorn Theatre), *Bullish* and *Joan* (Derby Theatre and Camden People's Theatre), *Magic Flute* and *Smallholding* (Soho Theatre), *Frontline* (Arts Educational Schools), *Witness* and *Words Unspoken* (National Tour), *Heartbeats and Algorithms* (Soho Theatre and National Tour), *Love Steals Us From Loneliness* (Camden People's Theatre and Chapter Theatre, Cardiff), *Stay Another Song* (The Young Vic), *Petrification* (Live Theatre, Newcastle, and Theatre503), *Greg Foot Tour* (National Tour and Leicester Square Theatre), *The Playboy of the Western World* and *As You Like It* (Southwark Playhouse), *Tonight I'm Gonna Be The New Me* (Soho Theatre and Forest Fringe Theatre), *Romeo and Juliet* and *The School for Scandal* (The Tobacco Factory, Bristol), *Beauty and the Beast* (Lowry Theatre, Manchester), *The Rivals* (Arcola Theatre), *Making Stalin Laugh* and *Listen, We're Family* (JW3 Cultural Centre), *Big Meal* (HighTide Festival Theatre), *Kreutzer Sonata* and *Orbital Motion* (Linbury Studio, Royal Opera House, Covent Garden, and National Theatre of Ireland – Peacock Theatre), *Lia's Guide to Winning the National Lottery 2012* (Bridewell Theatre), *Overruled* (Old Red Lion Theatre), *Man On Her Mind* (Charing Cross Theatre), *Song of Songs* (Royal Shakespeare Company) and *The Ugly One* (BAC).

Opera includes *The Magic Flute* (Hampstead Garden Opera) and *Sevastopol*, *Home* and *Roy Orbison in Cling Film* (Linbury Studio, Royal Opera House, Covent Garden).

Associate Designs include *1984* (Playhouse Theatre) and *4:48 Psychosis* and *Crave* (Crucible Theatre, Sheffield).

Peter Harrison | Lighting Designer

Productions at the Finborough Theatre include *Flowering Cherry*, *The White Carnation*, *17*, *Too True To Be Good*, *Japes*, and *The Very Nearly Love Life of My Friend Paul*.

Trained at Royal Academy of Dramatic Art.

Theatre includes *Pink Mist* (Bristol Old Vic and Bush Theatre), *Julius Caesar* (Guildford Shakespeare Company), *The Cardinal* (Southwark Playhouse), *Britten in Brooklyn* (Wilton's Music Hall), *Alfie White: Space Explorer* (Tall Stories), *Jerry's Girls* (St. James Theatre), *Much Ado About Nothing* (Ludlow Festival), *The Doubtful Guest* (Theatre Royal Plymouth and Palace Theatre, Watford), and *Bucket List* and *Translunar Paradise* (Theatre Ad Infinitum).

Dance includes *Jean and Antonin* (Gartnerplatz Theatre, Munich), *In Nocentes* and *Home Turf* (Sadler's Wells), and productions with Michael Popper, Intoto Dance, Ballet Central, and Urdang Academy.

Opera includes *Paul Bunyan* (Welsh National Opera), *Opera Works* (English National Opera) and *Orpheus in the Underworld* (Royal College of Music).

Associate Lighting Designs include *Written on Skin* (Festival d'Aix-en-Provence, France), *Made in Dagenham* (Adelphi Theatre), *The Commitments* (Palace Theatre), *I Can't Sing* (London Palladium), and *Collaborators* and *As You Like It* (National Theatre).

Alexandra Faye Braithwaite | Sound Designer and Composer

Productions at the Finborough Theatre include *A New Play for the General Election*.

Trained at the London Academy of Music and Dramatic Art.

Theatre includes *Room* (Theatre Royal Stratford East and National Theatre of Ireland – Abbey Theatre), *Kanye the First* (HighTide Festival Theatre), *If I Was Queen* (Almeida Theatre), *Rudolph* (West Yorkshire Playhouse), *Diary of a Madman* (Gate Theatre and Traverse Theatre, Edinburgh), *The Remains of Maisie Duggan* (National Theatre of Ireland – Abbey Theatre), *Torch* (New Diorama Theatre and Edinburgh Festival), *Simon Slack the Fantasist* (Soho Theatre and Edinburgh Festival), *The Future* (The Yard), *Happy to Help* (Park Theatre), *The Tempest* (Royal and Derngate Theatres, Northampton), *Grumpy Old Women III* (National Tour), *My Beautiful Black Dog* (Southbank Centre), *Butter* (VAULT Festival), *Boat* and *Feed* (Platform Theatre), *The Rolling Stone* (Orange Tree Theatre, Richmond), *Juicy and Delicious* (Nuffield Theatre, Southampton), *Cecilia* and *The Flannelettes* (King's Head Theatre), *Hamlet is Dead* and *No Gravity* (Arcola Theatre), *Fagin the Musical* (South Hill Park Arts Centre, Bracknell), *Remote* (Theatre Royal Plymouth), *His Dark Materials* and *Wind in the Willows* (North Wall Theatre, Oxford), *The Shelter* (Riverside Studios) and *Blackout* (The Castle Theatre, Wellingborough).

Associate Sound Designs include *The Glass Menagerie* (Nuffield Theatre, Southampton), *Dracula – Mr Swallow* (Soho Theatre), *Secret Theatre* (National Tour), *Glitterland* (Lyric Theatre, Hammersmith) and *Jumpers for Goalposts* (Palace Theatre, Watford, and Hull Truck).

Ailin Conant | Movement and Fight Director

Trained in Lecoq Physical Theatre at London International School of Performing Arts.

Theatre includes *Sugar and Spice* (Futures Theatre Company), *I Am Beast* (National Tour), *Bonnie and Clyde* (All In Theatre Company), *The Birds* (Ayyam Al-Masrah, Gaza) and *Sisters!* (Bakelit Art Centre, Budapest).

Direction includes *Nobody's Listening* (Bush Theatre), *The Marked* (Everyman Theatre, Cheltenham), *The Fantasist* (National Tour), *Nobody's Home* (Salisbury Playhouse), *Nineveh* (Riverside Studios), *Blue Butterfly* (Théâtre Pitoëff, Geneva), *Tachzor Shalem* (Cameri Theatre, Tel Aviv) and *The Caravan* (Beirut DC, Lebanon, in association with UNICEF).

Anoushka Hughes-Lewis | Production Manager

Trained at the London Academy of Music and Dramatic Art.

Theatre includes *The Good Person of Szechwan* and *Love Play* (Young Actors Theatre, Islington), *Tape* (Drayton Studio Theatre), *The Importance of Being Earnest* (Band of Others Productions) and *Directors Showcase* (LAMDA).

Opera includes *La Italiana de Algeri* (Pop-Up Opera).

Exhibitions and Installations include *Art of Make Believe Interactive Exhibition* (National Theatre) and *The Halloween Project*.

Rachel Graham | Stage Manager

Productions at the Finborough Theatre includes *Magnificence.*

Trained at Rose Bruford College of Theatre and Performance.

Theatre includes *Posh* and *Pyjama Game* (Pleasance London), *Cinderella* (First Family Entertainment), *Down to Margate* (Theatre Royal Margate), *Sweeney Todd* (Royal Academy of Music) and *Sister Act* (Lyceum Theatre, Crewe).

W14 Productions | Producer

W14 Productions was founded by Annabel Williamson in 2014 with a focus on new writing. Recent productions include *The Brink* (a co-production with Orange Tree Theatre, Richmond) and *The Late Henry Moss* and *Upper Cut* (Southwark Playhouse).

Production Acknowledgements

Jam has been generously supported by Arts Council England, The Carne Trust and Inland Homes.

Thank you to English Touring Theatre, the London Academy of Music and Dramatic Art, Amelia Bennett, Jennifer Bakst, Jane Claire, Ollo Clark, Katie Ebner-Landy, Ruth and Graham Fowler, Olivia Hanson, Phoebe Hames, Mariam Haque, Steve Harper, Emily Hickman, Emily Hitchcock, Luke Holbrook, Lowri Ifor, Carla Kingham, Zoë Lambrakis, Felix Legge, Jessica Siân, Lucy May Rothwell, Sid Sagar, Caitlin Shore, Sam Smith, Lyndsey Turner, Emma Waddington, Chelsea Walker, Patrick Walshe McBride, Rachel Wilkie, Harriet Wood, and Stephen and Jenny Wicks.

FINBOROUGH | THEATRE

VIBRANT **NEW WRITING** | UNIQUE **REDISCOVERIES**

"**Probably the most influential fringe theatre in the world.**" *Time Out*

"**No small theatre in Britain has a larger impact on the theatrical ecology than the tiny Finborough in Earl's Court… Even the National and Royal Court are hard pressed to make as many discoveries (or rediscoveries) as it routinely does**" Mark Shenton, *The Stage* – Top Venues 2016

"**The tiny but mighty Finborough…one of the best batting averages of any London company**" Ben Brantley, *The New York Times*

Founded in 1980, the multi-award-winning Finborough Theatre presents plays and music theatre, concentrated exclusively on vibrant new writing and unique rediscoveries from the 19th and 20th centuries. Our programme is unique – never presenting work that has been seen anywhere in London during the last 25 years. Behind the scenes, we continue to discover and develop a new generation of theatre makers – most notably through our annual festival of new writing – *Vibrant – A Festival of Finborough Playwrights*.

Despite remaining completely unsubsidised, the Finborough Theatre has an unparalleled track record of attracting the finest talent who go on to become leading voices in British theatre. Under Artistic Director Neil McPherson, it has discovered some of the UK's most exciting new playwrights including Laura Wade, James Graham, Mike Bartlett, Jack Thorne, Simon Vinnicombe, Alexandra Wood, Nicholas de Jongh and Anders Lustgarten; and directors including Blanche McIntyre, Robert Hastie and Sam Yates.

Artists working at the theatre in the 1980s included Clive Barker, Rory Bremner, Nica Burns, Kathy Burke, Ken Campbell, Jane Horrocks and Claire Dowie. In the 1990s, the Finborough Theatre first became known for new writing including Naomi Wallace's first play *The War Boys*; Rachel Weisz in David Farr's *Neville Southall's Washbag*; four plays by Anthony Neilson including *Penetrator* and *The Censor*, both of which transferred to the Royal Court Theatre; and new plays by Richard Bean, Lucinda Coxon, David Eldridge, Tony Marchant and Mark Ravenhill. New writing development included the premieres of modern classics such as Mark Ravenhill's *Shopping and F***king*, Conor McPherson's *This Lime Tree Bower*, Naomi Wallace's *Slaughter City* and Martin McDonagh's *The Pillowman*.

Since 2000, new British plays have included Laura Wade's London debut *Young Emma*, commissioned for the Finborough Theatre; two one-woman shows by Miranda Hart; James Graham's *Albert's Boy* with Victor Spinetti; Sarah Grochala's *S27*; Peter Nichols' *Lingua Franca*, which transferred Off-Broadway; Dawn King's *Foxfinder*; and West End transfers for Joy Wilkinson's *Fair*; Nicholas de Jongh's *Plague Over England*; Jack Thorne's *Fanny and Faggot*; and Neil McPherson's Olivier Award nominated *It Is Easy To Be Dead*. The late Miriam Karlin made her last stage appearance in *Many Roads to Paradise* in 2008.

UK premieres of foreign plays have included plays by Brad Fraser, Lanford Wilson, Larry Kramer, Tennessee Williams, the English premiere of Robert McLellan's Scots language classic, *Jamie the Saxt*; and three West End transfers – Frank McGuinness' *Gates of Gold* with William Gaunt and John Bennett; Joe DiPietro's *F***ing Men*; and Craig Higginson's *Dream of the Dog* with Dame Janet Suzman.

Rediscoveries of neglected work – most commissioned by the Finborough Theatre – have included the first London revivals of Rolf Hochhuth's *Soldiers* and *The Representative*; both parts of Keith Dewhurst's *Lark Rise to Candleford*; *The Women's War*, an evening of original suffragette plays; *Etta Jenks* with Clarke Peters and Daniela Nardini; Noël Coward's first play, *The Rat Trap*; Charles Wood's *Jingo* with Susannah Harker; Emlyn Williams' *Accolade*; Lennox Robinson's *Drama at Inish* with Celia Imrie and Paul O'Grady; John Van Druten's *London Wall* which transferred to St James' Theatre; and J. B. Priestley's *Cornelius* which transferred to a sell out Off Broadway run in New York City.

Music Theatre has included the new (premieres from Grant Olding, Charles Miller, Michael John LaChuisa, Adam Guettel, Andrew Lippa, Paul Scott Goodman, and Adam Gwon's *Ordinary Days* which transferred to the West End) and the old (the UK premiere of Rodgers and Hammerstein's *State Fair* which also transferred to the West End, and the UK premiere of Jerry Herman's *The Grand Tour*), and the acclaimed 'Celebrating British Music Theatre' series.

The Finborough Theatre won *The Stage* Fringe Theatre of the Year Award in 2011, *London Theatre Reviews'* Empty Space Peter Brook Award in 2010 and 2012, the Empty Space Peter Brook Award's Dan Crawford Pub Theatre Award in 2005 and 2008, the Empty Space Peter Brook Mark Marvin Award in 2004, and swept the board with eight awards at the 2012 OffWestEnd Awards. It is the only unsubsidised theatre ever to be awarded the Channel 4 Playwrights Scheme bursary ten times.

www.finboroughtheatre.co.uk

FINBOROUGH | THEATRE

VIBRANT NEW WRITING | UNIQUE REDISCOVERIES

118 Finborough Road, London SW10 9ED

admin@finboroughtheatre.co.uk | www.finboroughtheatre.co.uk

The Finborough Theatre has the support of the Channel 4 Playwrights' Scheme, sponsored by Channel 4 Television and supported by The Peggy Ramsay Foundation.

The Finborough Theatre is a member of the Independent Theatre Council, the Society of Independent Theatres, Musical Theatre Network, The Friends of Brompton Cemetery and The Earl's Court Society; and supports #time4change's Mental Health Charter.

Supported by

Mailing

Email admin@finboroughtheatre.co.uk or give your details to our Box Office staff to join our free email list.

Feedback

We welcome your comments, complaints and suggestions. Write to Finborough Theatre, 118 Finborough Road, London SW10 9ED or email us at admin@finboroughtheatre.co.uk

Playscripts

Many of the Finborough Theatre's plays have been published and are on sale from our website.

On Social Media

 www.facebook.com/FinboroughTheatre

 www.twitter.com/finborough

 finboroughtheatre.tumblr.com

 www.instagram.com/finboroughtheatre

 www.youtube.com/user/finboroughtheatre

Friends

The Finborough Theatre is a registered charity. We receive no public funding, and rely solely on the support of our audiences. Please do consider supporting us by becoming a member of our Friends of the Finborough Theatre scheme. There are four categories of Friends, each offering a wide range of benefits.

Richard Tauber Friends – Mark Bentley. Mary Hickson. Richard Jackson. John Lawson. Peter Lobl. Kathryn McDowall. Barry Serjent. Lavinia Webb. Stephen Winningham.

Lionel Monckton Friends – Stuart Ffoulkes. Philip G Hooker. Martin and Wendy Kramer. Deborah Milner. Maxine and Eric Reynolds.

William Terriss Friends – Leo and Janet Liebster. Melanie Johnson. Paul and Lindsay Kennedy.

Smoking is not permitted in the auditorium and the use of cameras and recording equipment is strictly prohibited.

In accordance with the requirements of the Royal Borough of Kensington and Chelsea:

1. The public may leave at the end of the performance by all doors and such doors must at that time be kept open.

2. All gangways, corridors, staircases and external passageways intended for exit shall be left entirely free from obstruction whether permanent or temporary.

3. Persons shall not be permitted to stand or sit in any of the gangways intercepting the seating or to sit in any of the other gangways.

Matt Parvin

JAM

OBERON BOOKS
LONDON

WWW.OBERONBOOKS.COM

First published in 2017 by Oberon Books Ltd
521 Caledonian Road, London N7 9RH
Tel: +44 (0) 20 7607 3637 / Fax: +44 (0) 20 7607 3629
e-mail: info@oberonbooks.com
www.oberonbooks.com

A catalogue record for this book is available from the British
Library.

PB ISBN: 9781786822130
E ISBN: 9781786822147

Cover image by Rebecca Pitt

Visit www.oberonbooks.com to read more about all our books
and to buy them. You will also find features, author interviews and
news of any author events, and you can sign up for e-newsletters
so that you're always first to hear about our new releases.

To my parents, Rachel, and my friends from school.

Characters

Isabella Soroush
Kane McCarthy

Notes

Punctuation reflects their speech, not syntax.

Kane's dialogue has been written with a West Country accent in mind.

When the text is capitalised, it suggests the volume of the character's speech.

/   indicates the line's interruption by the following line of dialogue or action at this point.

—   indicates a character being interrupted or interrupting themselves.

… may suggest that the words are trailing off, or that the character is struggling for words.

i.

Both paused in shock.

BELLA stood rigid near her desk, barefoot, in going-out clothes, wielding a heeled shoe; KANE waiting in the doorway in a light jacket, a large rucksack on.

They are in a classroom in an upper state school on the edge of a small town. It is early evening. Summer is coming.

BELLA. I – Yes, I remember you.

Kane.

They pause.

KANE. Goin' out?

BELLA. Sorry?

KANE. Goin' out?

She hesitates –

In town?

'ere, or –?

Not drinkin', surely. Drinkin'? You drink?

On Thursday pfff tha's; I mean pfff tha's –

Tired tomorrow, Miss.

Beat.

Like, pub or, club or –

Thursday's Lizard, innit? If yer –

No, 's Firestation. Firestation.

Tha'll be fun, Miss. Tha'll be –

There somethin' wrong wi' that 'eel?

Beat.

Jus' you wanna watch, Miss. If i's – Wi' tha' 'eight. I seen women go down 'ard. On the stairs like, a' Firestation. Slippery. Totterin', then …

BELLA. Very helpful of / you.

KANE. Bang; hah.

They pause.

BELLA. Kane it's nice to / see you but –

KANE. New lot; old lot; mix?

BELLA. I have to be, / have to be going.

KANE. I'd bet new. New? New?

BELLA. I don't …

KANE. Teachers. Mates. Teacher-mates. Mates who're –

BELLA. Yes, okay, I / understand.

KANE. I bet i's yer new lot 'cause, 'cause I doubt the old lot'd want anythin' t'do with you, right?

This bein' the rival.

You know that? You not know that? / 'ow'd you not –?

BELLA. I just don't understand / what you're saying.

KANE. I's i's i's – the rival, the rival school, this one is, to our old one. The schools 'ave a rivalry; this 'n' our old one. Rivals. They don' like each other. They argue; 'ave tiffs. They –

BELLA. Alright, okay.

KANE. I can' believe you don' – 'ow' you not know 'bout the rivalry?

They called us names. Laughed, gen'rally. Thought they was – this lot – yer lot – so much be'er –

We 'ad wars. 'uge bloody ba'les, on the fields, fer like, 'onour; surely you teachers knew a' least tha' …

'n' 'ere I find you on the other side: a traitor.

Beat.

/ BELLA moves around her desk and gets her bag.

BELLA. Actually Kane I'm on my way out.

KANE. I jus' got 'ere.

BELLA. I'm sorry, I really / have to go.

KANE. I wanna talk.

She hesitates –

BELLA. What for?

KANE. Jus' 'cause.

BELLA. "Just 'cause"? About what?

KANE. Everythin'; us.

Beat.

He goes to perch –

BELLA. Don't sit.

KANE. No, yeah; these tables; not much –

BELLA. The school is closed; I'm leaving.

KANE. Yeah everythin's bloody locked out there Miss; –

BELLA. Exactly.

KANE. I 'ad to climb this 'uge gate 'n' actu'lly think I caught my –

BELLA. Kane you can't be here.

They pause.

KANE. / Miss …

BELLA. How did you – No, how did you know I was here?

KANE. Yers was the only light on in the –

BELLA. No – here, now.

KANE. Well yer 'ouse was all empty, so I –

BELLA. My house?

They pause.

KANE. 'member Alan? Diffey? 'e works a' a shop few streets over. Seen you. Told me.

BELLA. Kane I'm going to leave now.

KANE. No you can't; we –

BELLA. Am I going to have to / call the police?

KANE. Come on, Miss …

BELLA. Okay, alright, I'm calling the –

KANE. No police.

Little pause.

Why'd'you … even … say tha'. I'm jus' … poppin' by; I jus' popped by / 'n' yer –

BELLA. There are people around.

KANE. Right?

BELLA. In the houses.

KANE. Sure.

BELLA. If I scream –

KANE. Why'd you scream Miss? Christ I'm – I jus' wanna …

He takes off his bag, slowly. She follows it with her eyes.

I jus' wanna chance / to talk.

BELLA. Is that …

… a baseball bat?

Her eyes are on a handle poking out of the top of the bag.

KANE. Oh … no?

BELLA. Let me out …

KANE. But –

BELLA. Just let me out …

KANE. No but –

BELLA. Let me out now or I'll …

KANE. I's, I'm –

BELLA. I'm telling you one last time –

KANE. I'm dyin'.

BELLA. Let me out or I'll – …

A pause.

KANE. D'you 'ear me?

They say I've got, uh …

He clears his throat.

say I've got 'bout six months; yeah.

I's uh, i's uh; ain' much they can do for me, see.

Been goin' 'ospital like, ev'ry few weeks. Reg'lar tests. They can 'ave me in 'ventually – 'ospice, but … said I wan'ed stay out. To the end.

No use jus' bein' bed; not tha' goin' bed fer few months don' sound some ways 'ppealin'.

's important I stay active; tha' I'm …

So I'm leavin'. Few days. Goin', travellin'. Tha's why I need to –

Don' know where yet, travellin'. Jus', set off. See where I … end up – Maybe Japan –

9

Why I need to …

Christ I 'a'n' really said this; i' like this. Makin' me … –

I feel i'. I's got me shakin'.

I'm, I'm – Yeah lookin' at the end 'ere.

Beat.

BELLA snorts.

Sorry?

She's laughing.

Wha's that?

She laughs, openly, at length. She drops her bag; her stuff spills out; she keeps the heel.

BELLA. Unbelievable.

You're – Yeah? You're – Great, great. Just great.

She blows a big raspberry, middle fingers up.

Right?

KANE. Okay.

BELLA. What I say to that.

KANE. Tha's clear.

BELLA. I hope your bollocks drop off.

KANE. Lucky for you it ain't bollock cancer, Miss.

Slight pause. She nods.

BELLA. Very good, very good –

Got the story, got the face –

Are you a changed man? Do you have one last wish?

KANE. I's …

BELLA. Drop it. They can go now. YOU CAN GO NOW.

KANE. Who?

BELLA. Your mates. Or no, maybe it's the new generation; one of my classes; a snickering munchkin army; led by the great –

KANE. No one's –

BELLA. You come in a pack, Kane. Well they can leave now; your prank has failed. That's the end of it – their, video or – you've failed.

KANE. I's not a prank, Miss.

BELLA. Liar.

He stares. She keeps glancing towards the door.

What are you –? Actually think I'll –?

Not for one second swallow this.

Slight pause.

10 years. Still a troll.

KANE. Miss.

BELLA. Been waiting for this? Under your bridge?

KANE. No.

BELLA. Still lying at 24 … –

KANE. 23.

BELLA. That's no good, Kane. Grow up.

He stares. She watches the door. She refocuses on him.

What of. You're dying, what of.

He hesitates –

Come on; you're dying; what / of.

KANE. I's complicated.

BELLA. Sure it is; –

He clears his throat.

/ what of.

KANE. Brain tumour / …

BELLA. What was that?

KANE. Brain tumour.

BELLA. What kind?

KANE. Pineoblastoma.

BELLA. Which means?

KANE. I's on my pineal gland. Right in the core of my 'ead. Right in, right in – There's no way to point a' i', really.

She hesitates –

They showed me scans. Looked funny. Yer 'ead's all, in sections. The tumour, you can see it bloomin'; looks like a bubble' a milk in yer tea, 'n' yer like: tha's not my 'ead.

Slight pause.

So they can see the bugger but not ge' to i' –

Could try. I's such an advanced state they'd prob'ly jus' kill me anyway, is the thing.

So i's all … one way from 'ere. Sick, 'n' dizziness; no sleep, these 'eadaches … Makes me speak slow sometimes. I see stuff. My face feels, goes funny. 'n' I'm changin'. 'ow we – Mum thought I was actin' funny. Then after tha' I … 'm gone.

She hesitates –

All wha' Doctor Ramsen says, anyway. 'e is a Neurology specialist, jus' gotta trust 'im, I think. Not sure I / 'ave a –

BELLA. "Ramsen" – r-a-m-s-e-n?

KANE nods.

She pauses, watching his face. He stares back.

Turn out your pockets.

KANE. My ...?

BELLA. Your pockets.

He takes items including a phone and a lighter from his pockets, and turns them out –

She checks the phone. Pauses.

Take off your jacket.

KANE. Yeah?

BELLA. Just give it here.

He takes it off and gives it to her. She pats it down.

Give me your bag.

He huffs the bag over to her, wincing a little and rubbing his shoulder.

She checks the outside of the bag. She opens the bag and looks in; looks to him.

What're you on your way to a car boot sale?

He shrugs.

She reaches inside and fishes about, checking what's in there.

Oh –

She pulls her hand out, looks at it – it's covered in something.

What's –? It's sticky.

He shrugs.

Bag juice? Is your bag sweating or ...?

He shrugs.

... unbelievable ...

She wipes her hands. Pauses.

Why the bat, then.

He shrugs.

Why the bat, / Kane?

KANE. None of yer business, frankly.

She laughs.

Look jus' – 'ave i'. 'old onto i', tha's ...

He shrugs.

She draws the bat from the bag; sets the heel down; keeps the bat. Pauses, watching his face. He stares back.

BELLA. Last chance: where's the joke?

KANE. No joke.

BELLA. What's your game?

KANE. No game.

BELLA. I'll give you to 3 to tell the truth, and there won't be repercussions.

Slight pause.

1.

2.

3.

She watches his face. He stares back.

You're not going to ask me to euthanize you?

KANE. What?

BELLA. Are you?

KANE. Jesus.

BELLA. Well …

KANE. Miss yer dark.

She stares.

I jus' wanna talk 'bout us. I's important, I been told.
Dealin' wi' …

He clears his throat.

unfinished business.

Beat.

So jus' … a li'le of yer evenin'. Fer us t'talk. You can gi' me
tha', can' you?

They pause.

BELLA. You'll stay / over there.

KANE. Cheers, Miss.

BELLA. Listen. You'll remain in that corner. Won't flinch –
won't sniff – without my consent; you'll do your talking, then
be on your way; / and if hooligans burst through that door,
the first is losing an eye.

KANE. Alright.

BELLA. Yeah?

KANE. Any invaders 'it 'em all you like, –

BELLA. That's / a deal then.

KANE. won't be with me. Yeah.

They pause. He stares.

BELLA. Over there, then.

KANE. Yeah, no.

He goes to the corner, with his bag. Puts it down. Turns and looks at her.

A pause.

BELLA. Go on, then.

KANE. Yeah, no, –

BELLA. There staring at me like a, –

KANE. No course.

BELLA. Disney hyena. Talk.

He hesitates –

Then pauses. Looks to her; catches her eye; looks down.

He mutters under his breath. He's very stiff. He scratches one side of his jaw; then rubs it, as if warming it up.

She goes to speak –

He stamps suddenly – mutters a curse – still staring down. She pauses.

He seems frozen.

/ He looks up quickly, smiling.

KANE. Ey, you'll like this.

He goes into the bag and rummages around, wincing slightly.

D'you 'member …

He pulls a small box to the top of the bag, opens it, takes out a Pokémon card.

Pokémon?

She stares.

Staple of any kid's chil'ood they're in their twennies; why ev'ryone went to'ally men'al over the new game, I'd guess. Big in my primary, then 'gain Year 5 I reckon, then on 'n' off, on 'n' off – even in upper fer a few people – You know 'ow i' is, these things … time you got 'em out they're gone again.

He makes a sharp tutting sound.

/ *As he speaks, he takes the boxes to a table between them, and begins to get out Pokémon cards, Damage counters, etc.*

Prob'ly – def 'nitely my fav'rite, actu'lly out'a the toys I think; they're tactical, 'n' varied – y'know they can be weak or bigger 'n' stronger – evolved – 'n' slash 'em, or beat 'em, or drown 'em. I got some Japanese ones too? Can' read 'em but y'know, still pre'y … pre'y tidy, yeah. You know any Japanese?

She stares.

But i' was them wi' all the best games, wa'n' i'. Digimon – the aggressive cousins of yer Tamagotchis; Beyblades – I 'ad Beyblades in middle school, so tidy, got confiscated. Miss Arbor. Wonder if she still – 'cause they were real excitin', dunno if you – You used the –

BELLA. Kane –

He stares at her. She stares back.

KANE. You used the rip-cord on this launcher right to eject 'em, 'n' they'd smash into each other, 'gain 'n' 'gain, 'stroyin' each other. Dependin' the Attack Ring, Weight Disk, etcetera, they'd do diff 'rent things – customizable – broadly in like Attack, Defense, Combination 'n' Endurance styles. I 'ad Magnacore ones, metal ones – Swear I once saw i' take the top off a kid's finger – 'cause – little known fact – their spin: 1.5 to 2 times faster than the old ones.

Little pause.

Always wanted to play like War'ammer, Dungeons 'n' Dragons too, but never got a chance – Y'know, I wa'n' in wi' the nerds – Nerds 'ad their club, wore suits, wi' an 'ammer – a judge 'ammer – used one of the RE rooms for i' – like a ceremony, or – Was odd. I watched 'em. Through the window.

He pauses. Looks at the table.

Yer one on one, 'ssentially. 'n' you battle.

He gets a deck of cards.

17

You, uh, shuffle …

He shuffles his deck. Then hers.

Take seven cards from the top of each of the, decks, 'n' put 'em face down.

He does so.

He takes three cards from each deck.

Three cards from each deck – they're prize cards. You don' need t'know these now, these're jus' the basics – but – Now put these t'one …

He puts them to one side.

Then the …

He puts the rest of the decks to one side.

Then you look at yours.

He looks at his own set of seven cards.

You –

He turns hers over, shielding his eyes.

You need a basic Pokémon. A' least one.

Pick an active Pokémon for 'ere. Then two fer the bench.

He lays his out in a triangle, face down.

Then we'd flip 'em over, consider 'ow to deploy 'em, but obviously you'd need t' … I shoul'n' … Anyway, this is a, demonstration.

He arranges her cards randomly, without seeing them. Then he flips his over. Then he flips hers over.

Now we could attack.

I got a Grimer, see?

'n' – Oh, oh okay; you've got a Charizard Shiny. Tha's really tidy. Di'n' know I'd put i' in there; i's actu'lly worth like – somethin'; was jus' my fav'rite, too. Always jealous 'cause, y'know, William Beech 'ad one. Maybe this is 'is? Might'a stole i'? Past now; anyway –

He clears his throat.

A majestic 'n' powerful creature. 's got i's, "fire spin". Burns them. Means the other person loses some – throws away their, energy cards. 'ventually actu'lly you can actu'lly throw bombs if uh – No you don' 'ave to though, tha's not required course.

A little pause. He clears his throat.

"Known to unintentionally cause forest fires". Bit of' 'umour.

He shows it to her.

See?

She takes it, not looking at it, staring at him. Beat.

Don't tear it up.

I mean – 'ave i' – Suits you – I don' –

BELLA. Kane.

Do you need some water?

KANE. Actu'lly tha' might be … yeah.

She goes to her bag, pocketing the Charizard as she does so; he sees this, goes to speak, stops himself.

She gets a bottle of water out of her bag, and brings it to him. He takes it.

Cheers.

'n' Miss? Le' me jus' say: I don' think you've aged a day. You coul' still be … 38, easy.

She stares. Walks back to her desk.

19

He drinks, glancing at her. She puts on a comfy shoe, glancing at him.

She can't find the other shoe. He sees; glances about; sees it – it's rolled near-ish him, under a table.

He goes and squats and picks it up. Shows it to her. She comes over for it.

He holds it out as if to put it on her; she pauses.

Puts her hand out. He gives her the shoe. She waits. He returns to his corner.

He has more water, glances around the room, avoiding her gaze. Then he begins to explore it a little, his corner at first, but branching steadily out. He glances to her periodically.

's not a shit 'ole, is i'. Still state bu' i's, like, shiny; much shinier – less dusty. More colourful.

Mean maybe could'a guessed, right, this area bein' – Y'know i's nice – Nicer town, mind, than mine, too – Be' they're be'er wi' you roun' 'ere, ey –

BELLA. What's that mean?

KANE. Huh?

BELLA. That they're "better –"

KANE. The kids. 'xpect they're nicer.

Slight pause.

Bu' y'know wha' I mean – 's outside, 's well. I' jus' looks bigger, fancier – bi' like a castle, I thought, up 'ere, fields below. Why is tha'?

BELLA. To keep the angry townsfolk out.

KANE. Wha'? No I mean 'cause, 'cause –

Ah but yeah you still got, look, bit where door 'andle 'its the wall. No stopper.

He makes a sharp tutting sound.

'n' these chairs. School, chairs. Kind'a, bit like 'oldin' a
blast'a cold air. Why they so light? Sometimes think I could,
like, jus' crush 'em like ...

BELLA. Mm.

KANE. But broadly, cleaner. Brighter. 'n' sturdier, I'd say ...

He raps a wall. Looks to her.

BELLA. Sure.

KANE. Right?

Mean our old place, i'd be ...

Tables – tops 'n' their bellies – 'ld be covered with the
most 'sgustin' stuff. You 'member?

BELLA. Almost lumpy.

KANE. Mean you still got – Can' stop kids; but nothin' like –

BELLA. The kind of things you wrote.

KANE. 'n' stuck under there. If I'm 'onest.

'n' there'd be a big dent in the wall there –

BELLA. You with that spanner.

KANE. Yeah; 'n' jus' more dents 'n' cracks in the walls
gen'rally, i' the old place, ... though maybe they got someone
into redo i' now, I dunno.

She shrugs.

'n' tha', tha' blue carpet tha' was like, thick – tall – Velcro –
seemed to, grab at you ... wi' black gum patches, 'n' frizz, 'n' ...

'n' great stained lockers. All down tha' wall. Bright yellow.
'sgustin'. Made out'a tha' thin metal slides up yer nail yer not
lookin'. 'urts like ...

BELLA. Yeah ...

KANE. Yeah ... you 'ad i', you know.

Slight pause.

No, i's … very … –

I mean le's not even compare my other place, my new place – if I tol' you i' was like bein' schooled in Satan's crack, I'd be feedin' you 'oney –

So congratulations. Well done.

BELLA. Thank you.

KANE. Seen yer 'ead of year 's well; wow tha's …

He gives her a little applause.

BELLA. Well … it's not …

KANE. I's good. Should be proud.

Wha' you teach now? Still 'istory?

BELLA. Yeah.

KANE. Like wha'? Wha' bits? 'torians? You still do 'torians?

BELLA. "Victorians"? With my Year 9s.

KANE. Yeah tha's when we done i', ey.

God I reckon ev'ryone does 'torians. Schools 'sessed wi' 'em. Maybe, maybe 'cause they're strict, ey. Strict bunch.

BELLA. Corporal punishment …

KANE. Yeah 'and-whackers 'n', 'n' – orphans 'n' stuff, y'know.

I see you like 'em …

BELLA. I do.

KANE. Yeah … Yeah … know you do.

Slight pause.

Know wha' I miss? 'sign-Tech. I was good a' tha'. Much better 'n 'istory. Mr Papkin, 'e'd tell me tha' a lot – bloody saint tha' man – I miss 'im, actu'lly. Actu'lly miss 'im. 'i'n tha' …

Who else'd I 'ave Year 9 ...? Mr Richards. God, Mr
Richards, 'e was ... 'e was mega. There was this one time, 'e
gave us pig 'eart to touch – so tough – 'n' we all stuck our
fingers in i' a' once, like zombies; 'n' we pulled 'n' tore i' into
scraps. 'n' 'e di'n' even mind; di'n' bat an eyelid; what a legend;
Mr Richards ... Mr Richards ...

Yeah I actu'lly got on wi' some teachers, ahah.

BELLA. Well ...

KANE. No yeah I'm not sayin' i' was an 'ouse-on-fire style
type'a situation, bu' still. Got on. A bit. Wi' them a' least.

'cause – see – wha' I reckon, right, i' was tha' they gave me
benefit the doubt. 'spite my ADHD, makin' me all – 'spite my
'sslexia – 'spite, le's face i', I coul' be a twat.

BELLA. You could.

KANE. Yeah I coul'; right twat me, sometimes, a' 13 – Think
anyone woul' tell you – fam'ly too – 'special', even – Mum,
Dad and Cherry – 'ands up: I was a twat.

He pauses.

You do a Model UN 'ere?

She hesitates –

BELLA. Yeah, I run one.

KANE. Always wish I'd done tha'. Dunno why. Sounded
def'nitely borin', but ... Would've liked to be Japan or
some'in', I guess. Dunno. My new place di'n' 'ave no Model
UN. Di'n' 'ave many models any kind ...

Bet yer glad I di'n'. Come 'long.

She shrugs.

Yeah, bet you are. Bet you / are.

BELLA. That might've been nice.

KANE. No, no.

BELLA. Yeah, why not? If you'd've behaved, you could've had Japan. I'd've given you your pick of East Asia if you'd sat still, and I hadn't found any stink bombs in my –

KANE. Tha's the thing though, tha's the thing –

BELLA. I would've.

KANE. You def'nitely would've …

You 'member my pranks, though?

BELLA. I do.

KANE. 'ow many?

BELLA. Fair few, I'd say.

KANE. Like like like like – time I drew green tits on all the windows?

BELLA. Yep.

KANE. Time I put kipper in the striplight?

BELLA. Oh yeah.

I loved it when you just jumped out our window.

KANE. Excellent …

BELLA. Our first floor window. For no reason.

KANE. Not that you know, ey.

Wait no no no no no – time I told you Mr Kessler'd torn up my 'istory work book.

She hesitates –

Y'know, I said 'e was 'nnoyed a' me, 'n' chased me outside, 'n' tore up the work book, 'n' threw it in this puddle, 'n' stamped on it? 'n' I like, cried a bit? 'n' you, you wen' 'n' confronted 'im? Really? Ah, was, was crazy.

Mean to yer credit, 'e was an angry man. 'e 'ad chased me before. Must'a been pretty 'mbarassin', though, I'd 'magine ...

BELLA. Undoubtedly.

KANE. Shame you star'ed figurin' me out, ey. Cottoned on t'me. Too sharp.

Got the feelin' I 'ad a tell?

BELLA. You did.

KANE. Maybe my face?

She stares.

Wha' was i'? Wha'd my face look like? Go on. Go on wha'd my –

BELLA. I'm / not going to tell you.

KANE. Come on, Miss. Wha' was i'? Wha' was my face? Go on.

She stares. He stares.

Ahh. Blood from a stone.

Say you 'a'n' got any food, 'ave you?

BELLA. No?

KANE. Missin' dinner ... Mum was doin' big spag bol ... Should'a brought snack bu' I jus' ... shoom.

I can' ... –?

BELLA. What?

KANE. Like check 'roun', can I?

BELLA. For food?

KANE. Yeah. Kids might'a ...

BELLA. The cleaners've been in already.

KANE. I got a good nose, me.

BELLA. Be my guest.

He checks about.

KANE. You not 'xpect i'? The, piss takin'?

BELLA. Why should I have?

KANE. You bein' so new.

BELLA. But there's piss taking, and then there's …

She pauses.

You had a thing about my teeth, didn't you.

KANE. Oh yeah …

BELLA. My big teeth – remember these?

KANE. Big gnashers, yeah I – No I / mean –

BELLA. "Big gnashers", "gurt fangs", that's right, that's right. "Miss, you got such a great smile, must be your big teeth." "Did you have to have big braces, Miss, for your big teeth?" "Miss, you'll handle that apple just fine, I reckon, thanks to your –"

I remember being impressed, at first. That you were able to dedicate yourself so thoroughly to something. Shame I was marking you on History, ey.

KANE. 's a talent.

BELLA. And you always seemed to think my "big teeth" were a racial thing.

KANE. Did I?

BELLA. That I had big teeth because my Dad was from / Iran.

KANE. Iraq – What?

BELLA. Iran.

KANE. I thought …

BELLA. Yes you did yes you did yes you always thought Iraq.

You just kept saying – I think you wanted it to be Iraq.

KANE. Yeah …

Think I was jus', like, interested in i', y'know. As a, as a –

BELLA. Asking about my "big teeth". When I was off to pray. Where my "veil" was. When you'd been naughty, if I'd chop off your hand. Or your –

… always staring at my teeth never my eyes …

KANE. Wha' …?

BELLA. … gaze averted, bobbing, little shaved head angled down …

… juddering, trembling, in those strange explosions …

Each morning the hairs on my neck would rise as you made your way across the school field. I could go towards my door and feel something and through the little pane I'd spy you picking at the carcass of a free school meal bag. I should've left a goat chained to my desk. I should've brought holy water to lessons.

When we were in the room, when you were on me, you were on me. We'd know because the air, the atmosphere, would shift, and we'd all turn. And there you'd be. Like something possessed. Staring right …

He is staring. Beat.

KANE. Corr, thanks. You 'scribe all yer kids like tha'?

BELLA. No.

KANE. You don' 'alf make me soun' 'pressive, ey. Like a, like a … I don' even know wha'. Only 13, 'n', 'n', I was –

BELLA. Old enough to take responsibility for your actions.

Slight pause.

KANE. Yeah?

BELLA. Yeah.

KANE. 13, though.

BELLA. Still.

KANE. 's tough, innit. 'cause like yer not 16. Not even 15. Yer also not 8. Or 10. Or even / 11.

BELLA. You, were.

He pauses.

KANE. I thought I was sensi'ive, Miss. After Chantal got 'xpelled fer, like, those drawin's'a you 'n' stuff end'a first term, I made myself – I was real sensi'ive – I was all aware of i'. Yer – People bein' – I'd tell you 'bout the graffiti in the toilets, woul'n' I. I'd let you know if I 'eard an off joke round school.

Thing is tha' was wha' made you diff'rent, Miss. To other teachers. Wha' made you cool, I think. Like the only, I think – the only – def'nitely in school, maybe in the square mile – maybe the only Arab I'd ever met. Course I was gon' ask 'bou' i'. Miss Soroush the Arab. I was / curious.

BELLA. Do I have big / teeth?

KANE. I – What?

BELLA. Do I have big teeth?

Slight pause.

You always said they were; others said they weren't; it's hard to tell.

Look.

She bares them.

He looks.

Well?

KANE. Uh.

BELLA. How are they?

KANE. Maybe it was their whiteness. Made me think they were bigger.

BELLA. Yes but are they big?

KANE. No?

BELLA. No? Come closer.

He does. He looks.

KANE. I don't look at many / teeth.

BELLA. But you've seen teeth, other teeth; –

KANE. Sure.

BELLA. So if you had to say. Come closer.

He does. He looks.

KANE. When I came in 'ere, I di'n't / notice.

BELLA. So they're not billboard size, not visible from space; but are they big, bigger than other teeth?

KANE. Average teeth?

BELLA. Yes.

KANE. But average, is – Like, what is –

BELLA. Come closer. Look at yours. Yours against mine. Go on. Go on.

He looks at his in a reflective surface, and at hers.

You know you look too long they just seem weird. Pull your cheeks out, stare at the whole mouth – they don't look human.

They pause.

If you had to say.

KANE. Right.

BELLA. If you had to say.

KANE. Right.

BELLA. If you had to –

/ *He breaks away.*

KANE. Yeah; alright; I'd say so, might be; might jus' be their whiteness; might be jus' we keep talkin' 'bout i'; yeah, they look bigger – bigger'n mine.

Then I 'ave small teeth.

He gets some distance.

'ere we go.

He's found a lunch box. He shows it to her. She nods. He picks through the stuff. A pause. She watches him.

Oh yeah, Miss, look wha' I foun':

He brings a worn, crumpled piece of paper from his pocket, and holds it out. She stares.

He brings it over to her, she takes it; she has a read, he gets some distance, focusing on the lunchbox.

She looks to him.

BELLA. Yes?

KANE. One'a mine fer you.

BELLA. I know.

KANE. See the commen'?

BELLA. I've seen it.

KANE. "Is this a joke, McCarthy? Abysmal."

Slight pause.

BELLA. And?

KANE. I mean … bi' 'arsh.

BELLA. Maybe.

KANE. Bi' much?

BELLA. Perhaps.

I don't like to sugarcoat.

KANE. No you don', no you don' ...

Not bi' mean though?

BELLA. Um ... sure. Yeah. Okay.

Slight pause. He stares.

It'd probably been a long day; I was marking late at night ... / and –

KANE. Yeah no bu', bu' I got lots'n they're like, all like tha'.

BELLA. I marked late a lot.

KANE. Bu', like ... you were a bi' ... like tha', weren' you. Bit mean.

Slight pause.

BELLA. I can see why you might say that. It's been said. I can be tough.

KANE. You don' sugarcoat.

BELLA. I don't ...

Sometimes you're mean. Y'know. Sometimes you say mean things. Not deliberately. You're tired, it comes out. What do you expect? We're not monks; we slip, too; we're human. You try it. Before 30 plus kids. You're thinking survival.

KANE. "Thinking survival"? Pffff ...

BELLA. We all do.

KANE. Really?

BELLA. Yeah; what do you think we think like?

A secret from the Magician's Circle: we can think of you however we want. Townie, Fatso, Jail-bait; can even loathe you, if we like. We just have to teach your Kings and Queens.

KANE. Pffff ...

BELLA. Welcome back.

KANE. Bru'al Miss Soroush ...

BELLA. Sorry? "Brutal Miss ...?"

KANE. Tha's wha' we called you.

I' was all, i' was all, you was all like ... dain'y some'a the time.

BELLA. "Dainty"?

KANE. Yeah, brigh'-eyed. Bambi-like. Y'know, flashin' yer nice smile, 'ands like ...

Then you were like: blam; yeah? All'a sudden. Temper – up there – nex' second. We jus' coul'n' predic' you. Di'n' know wha' was next. You'd suddenly be screamin', ragin', cryin' a bi' even sometimes – bu' like this, this, this – rage-cryin'.

BELLA. Rage-crying's useful.

KANE. You was a real tiger. We were on tiptoes. Step outta line, li'le bi' ... you weren' 'avin' any'a i'.

I'd be natt'rin' ... not meant to, sure ... wham you'd pick me, fer a question. Lazer-like ... 'n' I'd be, I'd be like ... uh, um, – strugglin' –

BELLA. That's school.

KANE. Yeah, bru'al, bru'al –

One time, you actu'lly – you'd been markin', right, a' yer desk, you 'eld up some work, you read the first line, you said "who's that's?" "Who's that's?" You read a bit more, then "who's that's?" "Who's that's?" Ev'ryone jus' like: wha' ... 'n' i' was bloody mine. Yer point: i' was terrible. Bru'al, Miss, bru'al ...

BELLA. / I don't ...

KANE. Corr, i's all comin' back, innit. You ge'in' tha'? Waves. Mus' be the smell or the, or the, or the –

This other time, yer nostrils flared. Middle'a sentence. 'bout, 'bout, war or some'in'. You walked out, we waited, you came back – deod'rant can in 'and. Sniffed. Sniffed. Asked me to step outside wi' you. 'cause I was smelly. Bru'al Miss, bru'al … so bru'al, jus' bru'al.

BELLA. I don't remember those.

KANE. You wha'?

Slight pause.

BELLA. Perhaps you're confusing me with / another teacher …

KANE. No, no – i' was you, / I 'member; I 'member well.

BELLA. No but, no but I wouldn't –

Kane. Time can do that. To these – You –

KANE. I 'member i' though, I –

BELLA. Well I'm afraid you're wrong.

Slight pause.

Could it be the tumour?

He hesitates –

Or maybe you told them as lies once. And over the years they've … You've come to believe them.

He stares.

I am … hard but not brutal, so …

In fact I get Christmas cards from a number of your classmates. They'd send Christmas cards to "Brutal Miss Soroush" …?

KANE. Can I –

BELLA. No you cannot see my Christmas cards.

A pause.

How are your lot?

KANE. My …?

BELLA. How're the lads?

Callum Stevens, Steven Anchor, Robbie Marsh, Peter Bixley, and Brian Fisher.

KANE. Tha's right, Miss. Tha's right.

Don' see 'em no more, 'xcept Pe'er. No we drifted, di'n' we. After I 'ad to move schools. Los' touch.

BELLA. That's a shame.

KANE. I' was. I' was.

Slight pause.

Corr they was mad ones, wa'n' they.

BELLA. Just a little.

KANE. Right mad ones, to'al men'al cases.

They was the, we was the – not all'a but – The Mafia.

Mafia's wha' we used to call ourselves. Those who – Wa'n' jus' us doin' the rivalry bu' we di' a lotta the work –

You 'ave eggs; you 'ave eggin's? The school?

BELLA. Yeah?

KANE. Wha' 'bout condimen' bombs? Brigh' red, lumpy – like wi' peanut bu'er, ketchup, –?

BELLA. Yeah.

KANE. Tha's i', then. Tha's The Mafia – tha's the rivalry. I' is still – Bloody tradition, ey.

You really don' 'member i'? Rivalry? Pfff, tales I coul' tell you …

He starts to get closer to her.

We'd egg, we'd condimen' bomb; we'd stone – wi' jelly tots – people, in town. Challenge kids to boxin'. Write on peoples' cars. Threw some liver at the football team once.

BELLA. "An offcut they couldn't refuse."

KANE. Ahh. Tha's – Off the – From the – Tha's brilliant, Miss.

You'd'a liked the wars, I reckon – not the fis' fights – the food wars – they was be'er, they was … We'd ge' bus over, lunch time, come outta yer 'edges – ambush – jus', jus' 'stroy 'em. We once 'ad the biggest – jus' the biggest – down there, i' the Autumn – 'alf the county's lunch took to the air that day, 'n' each 'n' ev'ry child was drenched in margarine 'n' Wotsits.

A slight pause. He's quite close to her now.

I' is int'res'in' you comin' 'ere, Miss. You really di'n' move far a' all. Not far a', not far a' –

Ey you smoke?

BELLA. Sorry?

KANE. Smoke?

BELLA. I'm sorry?

KANE. Coul' never smell it 'fore.

Beat.

BELLA. Said you'd stay over there.

KANE. No we –

BELLA. Agreed.

KANE. You been –

BELLA. Will you stay over there?

He hesitates –

KANE. Can if you –

BELLA. Then stay over there.

KANE. Yeah if you –

BELLA. Stay over there.

He returns to close to his corner. Watches her.

KANE. Yeah … tha's wha' I 'member.

Tha', righ' there.

Sparks.

'n' tha' face.

Beat.

Say I can' 'ave one 'a yer smokes, can I?

BELLA. No.

KANE. I'm gaggin', Miss; jus' one.

BELLA. If you were to go outside …

KANE. Ahhh. Don' ge' rid'a me tha' easily.

BELLA. I never could.

KANE. You did though.

BELLA. Well …

A slight pause. He watches her.

KANE. Miss was I special? Was I special fer you?

She hesitates –

BELLA. "Unique"? Sure. If not, at least … –

KANE. Di' you feel you were drawn t'me.

Beat.

BELLA. Absolutely not.

KANE. Ah well I did ge' lotta yer 'ttention.

BELLA. Of course you did.

KANE. Normal 'mount?

BELLA. Yes.

KANE. No I'm jus', I'm jus' wondrin' cause I 'member you watchin' me a lot.

BELLA. Can you blame me.

KANE. No bu' wi' tha' look, there.

Slight pause.

BELLA. This look, here? I'm sure I gave you this look tonnes.

KANE. No bu' my first day. I 'member i' my first day, i' form. My first look a' you … yer eyes –

BELLA. I don't know what you're talking about, Kane.

Slight pause. He clears his throat.

KANE. Guess when I was young, I … no I di' not feel like … comfortable, wi' adults, right – "the adults." 'voided 'em, 'cause … I dunno. They were all, wolves till they weren't.

Bein' watched, bein' treated like tha' migh'a made me feel … I should attack first. Pre-emptive-strike, like.

BELLA. Ah …

Well I can't help that.

KANE. You can 'elp yer face Miss, I mean …

BELLA. I can't help you misinterpreting my face. I can't help, if I'm doing my job, that you take it … –

KANE. You gotta keep an open mind, Miss. You shoul'n' be lookin' a' me on the first day like my mum after I've broken all 'er –

BELLA. Well there we are.

Kane it's not my problem if your parents' behaviour made me seem hostile. I understand. I mean I met them and sure, I understand, but –

KANE. Wha's that mean?

BELLA. Well they're imposing people, no?

KANE has a physical reaction – faint but there – to BELLA's words. As it builds he seems to vibrate.

Parents' evenings your mum was bunched up like a prizefighter, knocking back everything I said about you two. Your dad only came to one and he gave me the stink eye the whole time.

KANE. I', i' – Doe'n' i', well – Depends wha' you said, right –

BELLA. I was only ever polite. And they were volatile.

KANE. No.

BELLA. Really? I mean I'm sure they're good people, but based on what I saw –

I remember your dad picked your sister up once after a trip, and she looked like she was arguing and he, I thought he, raised his hand in a way that she flinched. I thought. And I wondered if maybe she was a little scared of –

KANE. No. No they aren' like tha'. 'n' Cherry wa'n' –

His physical reaction eases.

You only seen 'em a' – stupid school stuff; meet 'em a' our 'ouse, you'd see.

The vibrations have gone.

They're gen'le. Inside. Got nice 'earts.

They're jus', big people. 'n' like Cherry says, big comes off as … I seen i', always comes off as …

He pauses.

38

BELLA. I just meant –

KANE. Bu' you, you – you were, yeah, 'ostile. No, more'n –
Waitin' fer somethin' bad t'appen, willin' it even. 'n' 'n' 'n' 'n' –

BELLA. Kane.

A slight pause.

You were one of those kids you see and you think, "you're
fucked". Swiss cheese blazer, permanent fidget, absent-angry
parents, trekking off alone towards the estates.

I'd seen you, I knew a little of your background – and
yeah, that was enough to guess how you might act. And maybe
I was waiting for that behaviour to come, sure, but I gave you
time – more than I had – treated your fairly – fair as I could –
tried to help you.

And of course you joined your gang.

KANE. Tha's, –

BELLA. Yes, you joined your gang, of awful hopeless boys.
And you hassled the other kids, daily. Abused me, daily.
Dragged us all down, almost to, almost to –

A pause. They watch each other.

/ He indicates the lunchbox.

KANE. Last'a this?

BELLA. I'm alright.

KANE. Suit yerself –

We gonna 'dress the elephant?

BELLA. What?

KANE. Look Mr Elephant in the eye or not?

BELLA. Pardon me?

KANE. Are we gonna talk 'bou' 'ow you tried t'kill me?

A pause.

BELLA. What's that?

KANE. You tryin'a kill me.

BELLA. No, I'm sorry, what's –

KANE. Come on / Miss …

BELLA. No, remind me? I tried to kill you? Have I dreamt these last 10 years? Am I in prison, in a prison / cell?

KANE. You should be. Any justice, you'd'a been. Gettin' fired … / barely a scratch –

BELLA. I wasn't fired –

KANE. You lef' the school, I 'eard, di'n' you?

BELLA. I went of my own accord.

KANE. You were 'spended.

BELLA. Yes.

KANE. Wi'out pay, I 'member.

BELLA. Yes; and they heard me out, they saw the reality of what happened, and decided to let me stay. And I decided to go.

KANE. Yeah, yeah. Mr Webber di'n' push you? All 'ush-'ush? 'cause they knew wha' you were tryin'a do?

BELLA. No.

He stares.

I left because you'd made it … Because you'd …

A slight pause.

KANE. You can admit i' now, Miss …

BELLA. Oh … –

KANE. Wha's the 'arm, Miss, sayin' i', now?

BELLA. You are / so full of it.

KANE. I' was tense, there was a real, a real tension 'tween us, i' got too much 'n' you tried to kill me; –

BELLA. Kane ...

KANE. I'd e'en say i's unnerstannable; I was a twat; I was a shit; there's no doubt 'n' you –

BELLA. Kane.

KANE. Why you 'spended first place then?

BELLA. I made the mistake of being in a room alone with you, with the, with the door closed.

KANE. No' 'cause you 'it me?

BELLA. They understood that.

KANE. No' 'cause you grabbed my face like a like a –

She hesitates –

Yeah, yeah; yeah, yeah – truth's comin' out. Truth's comin' –

BELLA. You grabbed my hand.

Slight pause.

KANE. / No ...

BELLA. Grabbed my hand, pulled it to your mouth and – Look, your dental records –

She shows the scarred webbing of her right hand.

So hard you almost tore the webbing off. I had to get a tetanus shot.

KANE. No tha's wha' you tol' them. Tha's wha' you tol' – wha' you lied – bu' tha's not, tha' is not, as I said, as I tol' 'em, wha' –

You tried to brain me. Smash my skull in wi' this, this jagged –

BELLA. Jagged?

KANE. massive, sharp, metal / thing.

BELLA. It was a penholder; no yeah someone left a, a medieval weapon in a classroom, right.

KANE. I' den'ed the wall. Bounced over 'n' –

BELLA. It was a piece of plastic; –

KANE. Me'al.

BELLA. It was – anything – to hand, I was –

KANE. You lifted i' li' tha' – 'n' brought i' down li' tha' – jus' missed my 'ear – I 'eard i' whistle – 'n' i' wen' crack on my shoulder – I was seein' / stars.

BELLA. You were fine.

He hesitates –

KANE. I, I, I, I – only 'cause I was –

BELLA. You were up and coming for me, weren't you.

KANE. You 'it a child. Yeah?

You 'it a child 'n' tha's, 'n' tha's –

'n' I am adamant. Adamant. Adamant. You 'it me first; 'n you grabbed my face; 'n, yeah, I bi' you – 'n' I'm glad, you bloody 'served i' – You 'it me first, you 'it me first no question.

BELLA. I guess that's something we can't ever know; but –

KANE. 'ey. 'ey. No. There are facts, 'ere. No ma'er wha' school believed. Things tha' 'appened I am sure of – li' tha' you 'it; like tha' you 'it a child –

They know tha' 'ere?

She hesitates –

Mm, yeah. Dirty li'le secret, innit.

BELLA. I explained when I was asked. And they'd heard about you.

KANE. I don' believe you.

A slight pause.

I did a joke. A simple, 'armless joke. 'n' you took me to another classroom, closed the door, bullied me then tried to brain me when I wa'n' 'avin' i'. You lied to school; got me kicked out; sent to tha' shit-'ole two towns away; ev'ryone in town 'eard 'n', 'n' looked a' me 'n' Mum 'n' Dad 'n' Cherry like ...

BELLA. You shouldn't have assaulted me.

KANE. You don' even 'member i', do you.

BELLA. I do ...

KANE. I' don' e'en ma'er t'you, you jus', you jus' –

BELLA. I remember every inch.

Slight pause.

KANE. I bet you don'.

A slight pause.

Wha' was the weather? Tha' day?

BELLA. No, no –

KANE. Nice spring day, –

BELLA. I'm not / doing this.

KANE. 'til late afternoon when i' gushed.

Ah, see?

BELLA. We don't ... / You can't ...

KANE. Why'd you gi' Pe'er 'tention in form tha' mornin'?

'cause 'e was rude.

BELLA. Not ...

KANE. 'cause 'e said somethin' bad.

BELLA exhales.

KANE. 'cause 'e –

BELLA. Told a very offensive … joke. I remember that.

A slight pause.

KANE. When'd you ge' to the lesson?

BELLA. Like, two minutes late. I remember Danny by the door, Isla next. On the board … a drawing of a trench.

KANE. / Wha' was –?

BELLA. Which cheek did you smear your nosebleed on?

KANE. I' … i' … tha' one.

Wha' was the smells in the room tha' day?

BELLA. B.O. and egg –

KANE. Was always –

BELLA. Leaving the room there was a sound – from outside –

KANE. This, this, this grindin'. Tearin'. The builders.

Wha' was the light like?

BELLA. … cold, clear, little snatch of sun – walls looked, marble.

KANE. I was dippin' my knife in –

BELLA. Chutney –

KANE. Of which there were –

BELLA. Two types.

KANE. There was rollin' –

BELLA. Grapes.

KANE. Makin' cracker fer –

BELLA. Vicky.

KANE. Wrong, Chantal.

BELLA. Wrong, Vicky – Chantal'd left.

He pauses.

Hadn't been there for months. Went before Christmas, for the drawing – you said so yourself.

KANE. But ... No, I can see 'er.

BELLA. Well then.

KANE. No ...

BELLA. If you can see her ...

KANE. No, –

BELLA. If you've put her there.

KANE. I's, – I mean' Vicky.

BELLA. What is switching a few events around.

KANE. They 'ad similar 'air.

BELLA. What is, even, making up events.

KANE. I know wha' 'appened.

BELLA. Clearly you don't.

KANE. But, but, but, but – Why can I see 'er, though?

A slight pause.

BELLA. This is what I remember: you had them all there early. Waiting for me. By some strange magic. I walked in and I couldn't smell it, but I sensed it – my sixth sense, my Kane-alarm – you'd done something.

I waded through kids, right to the back; you were blocked by Brian Fisher's bulk; I could see your edges – especially your shoulder, which was pumping up and down, and I was thinking "surely he isn't, he can't be, he's –"

I got to Brian, and I peered round the long grass of his gelled fringe to see you. In your place. And despite the fact I'd been there two and a half years, behind you there was a banner saying "Welcome Miss Soroush". And despite the simple rule I'd given you so many times – no eating in lessons – Despite the fact I'd told you, specifically – I'd let it slip – not to ever bring it to my classroom because I hated, I hated, the smell of – You had before you, on the table, all laid out, a fully stocked artisanal cheese board.

Slight pause.

You were shifting some onto a cracker for Vicky. Your lot were lined up each side of you. And I stood before you and you glanced up – a little sheepish, a little proud, a little like Goldilocks at her porridge –

You said it's for me – you wanted to give me a proper introduction to your home with a taste of some of the local cheeses. You asked if I wanted some; I asked you into the corridor, snickering all around me. I took you into a classroom for some privacy; we chatted about your behaviour / – where you gave me all that blah blah blah as usual; –

KANE. ... you ...

BELLA. where you were a stone as ever. I told you to get your stuff and take the cheese to Mr Webber. And out of nowhere you said –

KANE. No ...

BELLA. I said "go and get your stuff" and you said "bitch".

KANE. ... you said ....

BELLA. You erupted – roaring at me, shuddering, up in my face your fists clenched –

KANE. ... I swear ...

BELLA. – you had a nosebleed, blood all smeared across your cheek –

KANE. … i' was you, you said …

BELLA. You said – You said – awful things. Vile, vile, terrible things, and – You came for me – I held off your face – You bit me – I threw you off – My blood was on your teeth – I saw you were coming for me again – Everything turned white hot – I, I reached behind me for whatever I could – picked that thing up and, and, just brought it down – to keep you away from me – so I could run.

She pauses.

And because I defended myself. Four of you came to my house one night; didn't you. Didn't you.

Yes; I knew you did.

I almost had you; I'm sure it was you. I was so – You cowards, balaclava-ed, bats drooping, fleeing into the garden, bashing through my patio doors like – squealing like – pigs – and I was right behind, gaining and I just – I almost had you – got your foot – when you were on the fence – I could feel the rest on the other side, pulling your arms – And I slipped. I slipped and there was a thump, in the field, and a yelp. And you got away. I pulled myself up to catch them dragging you off a broken tree trunk, stumbling away into the fields.

Police said they couldn't prove it, you had an alibi, but …

But I knew your scrawl; even in graffiti I knew it –

Knew those eyes. Glowing in the dark; your balaclavas couldn't –

Your smell; when I got home; I didn't hear you shredding my stuff I smelled you, your stink, all over my house; even the wind roaring through you stuck there; washing it all 10 times, moving house, still, you, clinging on – I could –

Your voice. On my walls. Your muck. In my bed.

She pauses.

47

Otherwise I might've thought the town was out for me. From the message dripping down my living room wall.

You assaulted me. Ruined my home. Came within an inch of destroying my career. You cry about having to move school? Most would've pushed for worse. I took pity on you.

And you actually come here. To my classroom. With a weapon. All casual. And suggest I have done anything to you.

What do you have to say to me?

What do you have to –

KANE. I' ... I' ...

BELLA. Just you try to justify it –

What do you have to say to me?

What do you have to say?

He's frozen; she snaps him out of it –

Hey – / What do you have to –

KANE. I ... I ... sorry.

BELLA. What was that?

KANE. I I I – sorry

fer fer

ev'rythin'; sorry fer ev'rythin'.

He pauses.

oh fuck

fuck why'd I

sorry I'm sorry. I'm sorry. I'm

idiot I'm a

should never've, never

no 'cause I am an idiot 'cause

oh I'm jus' 'cause

I been I been

jus' 'cause Cherry passed, 'n' I'm back wi' Mum 'n' Dad, 'n' i's all

BELLA. What?

KANE. work le' me go 'n', 'n'

I 'a'n' been right. Been wrong since Cherry passed

BELLA. Cherry ...?

KANE. I been plain wrong; I 'a'n' been right; 'n' I jus' thought ... I jus', I jus' thought ...

He clutches his head.

He goes and wretches over her bin. She watches.

He stops, and looks at her.

'eadache, Miss.

BELLA. Sit down.

He goes to the floor abruptly, sits. Then lies down.

They pause.

Do you have anything? For, for – this? Medicine or –?

KANE. I' my bag.

She brings the bag to him.

Cheers, Miss.

He tips it over and brings stuff out in handfuls onto the floor – school work, stationary, toys.

BELLA. Or I could call your parents?

KANE. This'll sort i'.

He brings out more stuff, then gets hold of what he's looking for –

Ah.

He brings out a bottle of vodka.

He starts to open it –

She comes and snatches it from him –

Miss – Come on.

She gives him the water; he drinks that. A pause.

BELLA. Does this happen often?

KANE. Jus' … le' me …

He lies there. She pauses.

Then she looks at the stuff covering her floor.

He splashes some water on his face; cleans the bag juice from his hands.

She sees a piece of jewelry. Picks it up. Holds it out to him.

BELLA. Is this –?

KANE. Yeah.

BELLA. When'd you –?

KANE. You lef' i' on yer desk like, November?

She looks at it.

BELLA. But this is silver. Does it not burn you?

KANE. Wha'?

She pockets it. Continues looking through the stuff. He watches.

She unveils some large stones. Lighter fluid. And a chunky metal penholder.

BELLA. Is this …

She picks it up.

... the one? The one I used to –?

KANE. Nah, one I made. We all made 'em. In Tech.

She puts it down – it lands with a thunk. She moves away from it.

BELLA. Why do you have all this?

KANE. I was goin'a burn it. Make a bonfire.

BELLA. Oh right. Yeah, course. Here or –

He shrugs.

KANE. Dunno. Somewhere. Maybe our old classroom, ahah.

She stares.

Anythin' won' burn is goin' in the sea.

He notices something in the bag. Pulls from it some crushed, wet supermarket flowers. Looks at them. Offers them to her.

BELLA. I'm good, thanks.

KANE. No, go on.

BELLA. Really.

KANE. Go on.

She hesitates.

BELLA. Who are they for?

KANE. Jus' Mum; I'll ge' more.

BELLA. Give them to your girlfriend.

KANE. Nah, go on.

She takes them.

'n' forgive me.

's wha' you do, innit?

Will you?

She hesitates –

BELLA. I don't need to, –

KANE. Go on.

BELLA. Just … forget about it.

He goes to kiss her shoe; she jerks back.

What're you …?

KANE. Kissin' yer shoe. Thought you might prefer tha'.

He looks up at her.

BELLA. Why would –

He goes to kiss her shoe again; she moves away.

No.

KANE. Suit yerself … But i's on the table, Miss.

A pause. She takes up the bat and plays with it.

BELLA. You feeling better?

KANE. Uh …

BELLA. How're you getting home?

KANE. Bus.

BELLA. Ah, you'll be fine then.

KANE. From town – bi' of a walk first.

A slight pause.

I'll jus' – I'll jus' ge' my bearin's.

BELLA. Okay.

KANE. If yer sure.

BELLA. No, it's –

KANE. Don' wan' you t'miss yer night out.

BELLA. I'm no longer in the mood.

KANE. Yeah. You gonna go 'ome, or …?

She stares.

Prob'ly be fine, but jus' in case: if I go down foamin' or my eyes go … put somethin' 'tween my teeth so I don' eat my tongue.

She nods.

Cool.

They pause.

BELLA. I'm sorry about Cherry. I didn't realise.

KANE. Ah, i's …

'appened couple months back.

She wa'n' 'appy.

BELLA. Your poor parents. With your diagnosis too.

KANE. Yeah …

Got me goin' therapy wi' 'em, so … 'n' church wi' Mum.

Cherry'd be so glad I was 'ere, though. Gave me such 'ell fer that stuff wi' you.

BELLA. Yeah?

KANE. Yeah. You was 'er fav'rite.

BELLA. That's nice.

KANE. She always tol' me 'ow you were nice 'bout 'er art stuff. 'n' le' 'er si' wi' you durin' breaks a few times. She said she thought you were someone she coul' talk to.

BELLA pauses. He watches her.

You got any fam'ly, Miss?

She hesitates –

BELLA. I do.

My parents, and two sisters.

KANE. Two? I'll bet yer ... youngest.

She stares. He taps his temple.

Where are they?

BELLA. London.

KANE. What they do?

BELLA. Barrister, academic, barrister, journalist.

KANE. Wow. Two barris'ers? Wi, wi' wigs 'n' –?

Wow. Wow. Wow.

You see 'em much, or are they too busy wi' their –?

BELLA. I see them.

KANE. You all do much ... Iraq / i –

BELLA. Iranian.

KANE. Iranian, stuff?

BELLA. Sure. We do some Iranian things. In London.

KANE. Cool. Cool.

D'you ge' on wi' 'em?

She hesitates –

BELLA. Sorry which bus was that you're getting?

KANE. 36. Why?

BELLA. No, I just ...

A pause.

KANE. We always thought you might be lesbian?

BELLA. Sorry?

KANE. Lesbian?

She stares. A little pause.

You gotta boyfriend?

BELLA. Kane I'm –

KANE. Oh …

He looks dizzy.

Sorry, sorry. Tha' was … I'll jus' …

No you were sayin', 'bout yer boyfriend?

She hesitates –

Long one?

She hesitates –

Ahhh, yeah you do. 'n' 'e 'a'n't put a ring on i' …

She stares.

Wha's 'e like?

BELLA. He's far as possible from this, and will remain so.

He once used Lynx and I said I knew a particular group of boys who fogged – absolutely fogged – themselves in that stuff and if you ever do again you're dumped.

KANE. … guess we know who wears the trousers …

BELLA. Sorry?

KANE. Wha's 'e / do?

BELLA. No. I'm not having that.

A pause.

He gets up, unsteadily, makes to leave –

KANE. I bes' le' you get back to 'im –

BELLA. Kane …

KANE. No I'm keepin' you from 'im, beau'iful Thursday night, i's monstrous.

He's wobbling.

BELLA. Kane just sit down.

He does. A pause.

KANE. Why were you still workin'? This time'a night.

BELLA. I'm a teacher.

KANE. Stuck i' this place till 's almos' dark, pfff … feel fer you.

You could be 'ome wi' the boyfriend, 'avin' nice dinner, bottle'a finest wine, chillin' by a fire in the garden …

Wha'? 's wha' you do, innit? Nice little place in country; goin'a rest'rants all'a time; cruisin' in in mornin' 'n' grabbin' a nice coffee in town …

BELLA. Not quite.

KANE. What'm I missin'?

Slight pause.

BELLA. / The chaos.

KANE. The affairs.

BELLA. Sorry?

KANE. Yer affairs. Teachers', affairs.

BELLA. Right.

KANE. We always 'eard murmurs.

Any chance you'd tell me … who?

BELLA. Who?

KANE. Was 'avin' 'em.

BELLA. We don't have all night.

KANE. Jus' the biggest. The mos' shockin'. Go on. Don' ma'er you tell me now, does i'.

BELLA. … Whaley and Steed.

KANE. Mr –? Mrs –? No way.

BELLA. Their partners left them. They've got a kid.

KANE. Pfffffffffff … Men'al.

Know wha' was always great? When i' went roun' a teacher was shaggin' a parent. Like Mr Kessler wi' Isla Rogers' mum. Trauma'ic. Isla's face. They met a' a parents' evenin'. Which don' seem sexy to me, but …

BELLA. You'd be surprised.

KANE. Yeah?

BELLA. No.

Slight pause.

KANE. Mus' be, mus' be – somethin' in the air, right?

'ard to say wha', though …

Slight pause.

He gets himself moving again – exercises parts. As he does so, he glances around, especially at her desk. She watches him, leaning on the bat.

He sees something on the desk – a cover letter – and pauses. Picks it up, reads the start.

Yer goin' fer Deputy 'ead, Miss?

BELLA. I am, yeah.

KANE. Wow.

Why?

BELLA. … a friend suggested it.

KANE. Deputy, then 'ead?

BELLA. Perhaps.

KANE. Then wha'?

BELLA. More schools. Bigger schools.

KANE. You not still wanna do somethin' else?

I 'member this lesson, see, Josie Ireland asked you 'bout bein' a teacher, 'bout whether you'd always wan'ed'a to be one. You 'member tha'?

She hesitates –

You, course, said no. But you also said you still di'n' know wha' you wan'ed properly to do ye', or somethin' like tha'.

'n' there was this 'ush. 'cause we all knew i' was the truth. Kind of respected you fer i'. Then Diffey star'ed laughin'. Then Chantal. 'n' we were all jus' laughin'.

I 'member 'cause you blushed.

BELLA. It's a good job.

KANE. Yeah no, teachin's –

BELLA. The Deputy role; of course teaching's – Teaching's a great job.

KANE. Oh, yeah, course – Mean I'd do i' if I could.

BELLA. Maybe you should, ahah.

KANE. Teach?

BELLA. Yeah, sure, why not. They'd probably hire you.

A pause.

KANE. You really reckon?

BELLA. Oh. You –? Seriously?

He hesitates –

KANE. Nah. Nah. I'm jus' ...

He pauses.

No yeah why not.

Well I mean –

No yeah. I would actu'lly.

BELLA. Why?

KANE. Dunno.

I want to.

BELLA. No but why.

He pauses.

KANE. Uh ... I ... guess stuff like ... wha' you did fer Cherry ... makes me think ... I woul'n mind tha' ... myself – doin' tha' – yeah.

A pause.

Stupid idea; stupid / idea.

BELLA. What about travelling?

KANE. Ah, tha' was jus' 'cause I di'n' know what else. 'sides I'd rather die 'ere, 'ome soil, than ... Japan.

BELLA. Maybe you'd be better off spending time with your family.

KANE. Six months? We'd all die.

BELLA. I mean if you want to use those last months ... –

KANE. 'xactly, I'd be usin' 'em.

A pause.

BELLA. I mean ... it's possible –

KANE. Yeah?

BELLA. Possible you could be a TA. An assistant.

KANE. Oh right?

BELLA. But there would checks. Like if you've been to prison ...

KANE. Yeah, sure.

I mean I 'aven'.

BELLA. Well a criminal record of any kind –

KANE. I'm clean. Untouched. Few close calls. Some gen'rous policemen takin' me 'ome by my scruff, but ...

A little pause.

BELLA. Your, issues, they might –

KANE. My ADHD?

BELLA. Sure; you presumably still have, problems? I'd imagine you're –

KANE. I still find i' 'ard to concentrate, sometimes. But I'm so much less 'yperactive; i's right down; my focus: zoompf. Like a, like a ... – I'm medicated. I practice, mindfulness. I see this therapist now. So I'm good, yeah.

BELLA. Great; any experience working with kids, though?

KANE. I've 'elped out a' Cubs and Beavers. Mate's Dad's Akela.

She pauses.

Would I need like, CV? I can make one'a those. I've 'ad jobs; I've 'ad so many jobs, me. Mos' recent, was workin' on the buildin' site. Shortly 'fore that, cleanin' at main 'ospital. Sometimes 'spensive 'quipment, sometimes the locked rooms even.

BELLA. ... far as I'm aware they can train you on the job. We like to see a little more, but ... I don't even think you need A Levels, maybe it's just / GCSEs.

KANE. I got A Levels.

Slight pause.

BELLA. Yeah?

KANE. Yeah. I got four.

BELLA. Four? Four's good. Where from?

KANE. Forsythe College. I wen' back. Felt like I should 'ave some.

BELLA. What in?

Beat.

KANE. D&T.

BELLA. Sure.

KANE. Geography.

BELLA. Course.

KANE. Biology.

BELLA. That a joke?

KANE. No.

BELLA. Suppose you've got a P.H.D too?

KANE. Jus' the A Level.

BELLA. That's three.

KANE. Yeah, fourth is Bricklayin'. Tha's an NVQ, but …

BELLA. Eclectic bunch.

KANE. … I don' …

BELLA. You always were an all-rounder. Didn't continue with your History, then.

KANE. No. Guess you put me off, Miss.

A pause.

BELLA. I think you could volunteer first, –

KANE. Alright.

BELLA. and maybe … if there's time … become a proper TA.

Someone might take you on for P.E. or something right away; I don't know.

KANE. Maybe you'd gi' me a reference?

She hesitates –

BELLA. Perhaps think about it some more, you might –

KANE. I know I could do i'.

Like what'd you do …?

In; quiet down.

Tell us few facts – pu' 'em on board – usu'lly like fun fact or some'in'.

Then you'd say "quiet readin' time". We'd read some'in'. You'd read yer novels.

Then you'd chuck us a past paper 'n' boom, lesson done.

Or pu' a film on, right a' the start. Either tha' one abou' rights or tha' one abou' dragons.

BELLA. I mean … we did a little more than that, but …

KANE. No but tha' was wicked, Miss – I loved tha' dragon film.

'ey, you ever make stuff?

BELLA. Like what?

KANE. Models, structures –

BELLA. No.

KANE. I could do tha'. My dad's got model planes, my mate's a carpenter.

You ever re-enact stuff? Battle scenes?

BELLA. No, but ...

KANE. I'd do tha' too.

'n' I'd do trips – I'll drive a minibus – I'd take 'em to the 'aunted bakin' place. The 'torian place we went where i' was 'aunted, 'n' you di' bakin' – No maybe tha' was primary. Anyway, still relevant, I'll take 'em to the 'aunted –

BELLA. Kane it's not ... There are ... You can't just ... It doesn't work that way.

KANE. Why not?

BELLA. It's all ... just ... –

When I had you – I was green – I thought exactly the same. And then you get in there and it's havoc and you're looked at like the wicked witch and little assholes like you take up all your time and you just want control and these ideas, these fun things – Not that half of them are even – they die.

KANE. Right ...

BELLA. I mean we do have some fun. Like FOFO lessons.

KANE. I don' –

BELLA. Fuck Off and Find Out. Independent research time.

KANE. Oh.

BELLA. They love that.

KANE. I bet.

BELLA. And I love that ... Oh how I love that ...

KANE. Why'd you do i' then? Make i' soun' shit.

BELLA. I like other things too.

Sports Day. I really like Sports Day. I mean partly it's just funny – all these misshapen kids pretending to be Olympians for seven hours – but also just the ... change in context. You see everyone differently; no one's at throats.

And results day. Their dumb little grins. Yeah ...

And, and, actually, some of the naughtiness – the right naughtiness – especially when I don't have to deal with it. The cheese board, I'd've found that hilarious, if it wasn't me.

KANE. I' was funny.

BELLA. It was and it wasn't.

KANE. 'ey: 'magine me, right, chuffin' i' 'ome fer the cheeses. I 'ad to chuff i'all the way down the field i' break, 'void my Mum, fill my bags wi' the cheeses, 'n' the board, 'n' the grapes, chutneys, crackers, knives, plates – 'nough fer like six people – 'n' then chuff i' back up the field, up tha' incline, wi' tha' bag, li'le me.

She laughs.

See. I was good a' pranks, you can' deny tha'.

BELLA. I couldn't, no.

Slight pause.

KANE. Ey, coul'n' ge' an A*, coul' I? Fer pranks.

BELLA. Sure. A* in Pranks.

KANE. My first A* ...

BELLA. I'll go one further:

She holds out the bat, near his shoulder. He stares at it.

Then she knights him with the bat.

I knight you ...

KANE. Oh Miss you shoul'n; King of, King of –?

BELLA. Knight of Pranks.

He bows. A slight pause.

KANE. 'ey, you really still get Christmas cards from my lot?

BELLA. I do.

KANE. Like who?

BELLA. Rachel Doorsley. Caitlin Carter.

KANE. She's a nurse at the 'ospital; used to see 'er when I was cleanin' there.

BELLA. Isla.

KANE. Really? Never thought she liked you.

's jus' she was always tryin'a gi' you extra work. Like whole extra –

BELLA. Like two extra assignments a week.

KANE. 'n' you were like: no thanks.

BELLA. No thanks, Isla. You're getting an A, we'll leave it there.

Well, I did help her get into university. And a placement at a paper through my sister. So ... I earned the cards.

KANE. Cherry ever send you one?

BELLA hesitates –

BELLA. I don't think so, no.

KANE. I thought she mentioned once she 'ad. Some of 'er art.

BELLA. One of her paintings?

KANE. Drawings.

BELLA. That's right.

A short pause. KANE begins to have his physical reaction.

KANE. D'you not ... 'member 'er?

BELLA. I remember things. But it has been a little while, Kane.

KANE. She said you were close.

BELLA. For teacher-student.

KANE. Wha' d'you 'member?

BELLA. Um ... She was a quiet girl.

She was – Yes, she was doodling all the time; and they were good.

She wanted to be a ... hairdresser.

KANE. No.

BELLA. Manager at your local –

KANE. No.

He's almost vibrating.

BELLA. I remember sitting at her with breaks. I remember talking. Then I remember you.

I've had so many kids, Kane, and you're probably numero uno, memory-wise, but there's still that ... fog. Isn't there.

His reaction begins to ease up.

I really liked her.

KANE. I know you did.

He takes a moment.

BELLA. You're looking much better. I reckon you can make that walk to town, now.

KANE. Yeah, sure.

BELLA. Great.

Much as I'd love to keep some of this stuff, if you could clear it up.

KANE. Course.

He begins to clear his stuff up, slowly. She puts the bat by his bag, then gets her stuff ready too. He seems more interested in looking at or playing with the stuff than putting it away.

Yer gonna go fer tha' job, then? Tha' Deputy one?

BELLA. ... yes.

KANE. Yeah? You don' sound so sure, Miss.

Why wouldn' you? Do i'?

BELLA. Ah ... It's more admin. Less teaching. So –

KANE. Less teachin', though. Fer more money?

BELLA. Yeah ...

KANE. Bu' more admin, though. 'n' maybe you wanna keep teachin'.

BELLA. Yeah ...

KANE. I's good to 'ave wobbles, I think.

She hesitates –

Though I 'xpect you know wobbles better'n I do. 'avin taught the likes'a me.

BELLA. Come on, bit quicker.

He loosely goes back to clearing up.

KANE. Be' i' was a relief when I went, ey.

BELLA. Oh yeah. Prayers-have-been-answered-style relief. Other teachers thanking me on their knees for ridding the school of you ... We had Cava in the staff room.

KANE. Really? Not champagne?

'n' you di'n' think: screw this. What if I get more like 'im?

BELLA. Well of course. I had fever dreams filled with civil service roles for weeks. But I wasn't going to quit off one bad experience. Even such a nightmare as you. Besides what else would I have done …

A pause. She checks her pockets, looking for something; finds the Charizard shiny.

Oh, here.

She gives it to him.

KANE. Thought you might be keepin' i' fer yerself.

He looks at it. Tears it up, casts the pieces away.

Tell you I dreamed, when I was li'le, I coul' play those fer work. Jus' those be my – Stupid.

What'd you wanna be? As a kid?

'ey, le' me guess: a barris'er.

BELLA. Yep, you … –

KANE. Why di'n' you do tha'?

BELLA. Not exciting enough for me.

KANE. So you could'a 'n' you chose not to? Wow.

Slight pause.

You never think'a still tryin'?

BELLA. No.

KANE. No?

BELLA. Come on; this is –

She helps him pack his stuff.

KANE. 's never crossed –

BELLA. The thought has crossed my mind, yes.

KANE. 'ey that'd be so impressive. 'avin' done both those. Like teachin': done tha'. Nailed tha'. I'm jus' off t'be a swanky –

BELLA. You don't just become a barrister, Kane.

KANE. Why not?

BELLA. Why –? It's hard. And expensive. And, and …

KANE. Yeah but you could 'andle tha'.

BELLA. I don't want to, though. I don't want to.

A pause.

KANE. Look, Miss. If I got any advice I can give. Any I got right to give. I's: don' waste time. 'cause there come a time when you ain' got no more time to waste. Like me. 'cause I'm almos' dead.

Seems to me you don' wan' tha' stupid Deputy job 'n' I think yer right. Wha' you wanna do paperwork even la'er a' night? You nuts? I was you I'd burn that application. I'd burn i'. Jus burn i'. You shoul' –

BELLA. I'm not going to –

KANE. You gonna 'pply fer i'?

She hesitates.

Tha's yer answer, frankly.

D'you unnerstan' wha' I'm sayin' gen'ral though? Wha'e'er you wan', do i' now, fer God's sake. Don' think abou' … lookin' stupid. Yer age. The past. Or, or money – Money's – Wha's money, yeah? Wha' even – Can' take i' with, can you.

So you wanna be a barris'er, you be a barris'er, Miss, you don' / le' –

BELLA. I –

KANE. No I think you do. Really. I can see i' in yer eyes – you wan' it; yer jus' scared. But don' be scared. Tha's crazy – I shoul' be scared – I am scared – I'm dyin'.

Jump. Jump. Jus' do i'. Yeah like, quit teachin', tonight,
'come a barris'er; why the 'ell –

BELLA. Tonight?

KANE. Yeah, tonight. Why not tonight?

BELLA. That's crazy.

KANE. Yer Miss Soroush, yer crazy.

What you gotta lose, anyway? You already done so much
good. Fer so long. 'ow many kids you reckon you 'ffected,
maybe 'undreds? Thousands? All o'er, prob'ly – all the country
– maybe the werld. Doin' good. 'cause'a you.

I reached this point. I'm lookin' a' my death bed. 'n' what
I gotta show fer i'? Fuck all. I done fuckin' nothin'. I may as
well, frankly, 've been dead this time; yeah …

Tell you I woul'n'a caused all the grief …

'n' like fam'ly; wha' I woul'n' gi' …

He pauses.

Wha' I woul'n – You got chance? Make up wi' 'em? Bad
feelin's? Take i'. You go 'ome 'n' you … You go 'ome – Back
to – 'n' you …

He pauses.

You got chance t'change you take i'. I woul'; I will, wi' …

He pauses.

Funeral, I was jus' … I was so sad, bu' … all I coul' think
was: this is so dumb. So stupid. 'er in this box. Name on some
stone. Us in this 'all. Sayin' stuff. No one anythin' 'pproachin'
Cherry – 'ow 'mazin' she was. I tried: jus' drivel. I'm thinkin':
'oly fuck, we're fuckin' this. This last thing. She'll be, jus', dus'
soon. Gi' me a li'le more – a li'le 'elp 'ere, someone … Bu'
course we di' anyway. Wha' di' I 'xpect? 'n' this'll be yours, too.
Yours'll be worse. 'cause i' won' even be a, a … 'er in the box.
I' 'll be the dumb fuckin' –

She hugs him.

BELLA. I'm so sorry. About Cherry. About all this.

KANE. No, tha's ...

... thanks, Miss.

BELLA. Bella. All this "Miss" is creepy.

KANE. Alright. Thanks, Bella.

You gonna take my 'vice, Bella?

BELLA. I ... I might.

KANE. Yeah?

BELLA. Yeah. 's good advice.

KANE. Really?

BELLA. Yeah.

... and I ... I'll give you that reference – if –

KANE. Really?

BELLA. If you figure out precisely what it is you want.

KANE. Cheers, Bella.

Her hand is resting on his shoulder. She squeezes the shoulder – he winces.

Ah.

BELLA. Sorry –

KANE. No i's – My shoulder's ...

He pauses. Then he whips his top off – he is naked from the waist up.

He has a number of tattoos, and a few scars. His shoulder is dominated by a long scar – he shows it to her. A pause.

BELLA. Is that from me? That day?

Surgery?

He nods.

But that's ... I didn't ...

She stares at the scar. Then touches it. He pauses.

She removes her hand. He clears his throat.

KANE. Gun show ...

BELLA. Some good tattoos you got there.

I like the ...

She indicates a blue dragon on his bicep.

Sign for the Chinese in town.

KANE. 'ey, i's cooler than tha': i's the logo fer the Beyblade TV series.

He turns around: there's an angel on his back.

BELLA. Oh wow.

KANE. Tha' one's fer Cherry.

She hesitates –

BELLA. Sort of worried you'd have my face on your back.

He stares.

KANE. This one's, sort'a, Cherry-inspired too:

He shows her a quote on his wrist: "too dead for dreaming".

BELLA. "too dead for ..." Dylan?

KANE. Cherry got me into 'im.

BELLA. Ah ... I used to have him playing in my first few years. While the kids were working. With Cherry, I'm almost certain.

KANE. Tha's ... I reckon tha's about when she got into 'im. No way. So you ...

BELLA. Guess so.

KANE. 's crazy.

I mean I love 'im so much I bloody learnt guitar. All 'cause'a –

BELLA. Really?

KANE. Yeah; Old Bob.

BELLA. That's great.

Since –?

KANE. Yeah I must'a been 12 I started.

BELLA. I expect you're good by now.

KANE. Well ... jus' a bit, yeah. Always been good with my 'ands, 'n' –

BELLA. I've tried before, to learn, but ... My boyfriend started teaching me, actually –

KANE. What grade is 'e?

BELLA. ... 7, perhaps?

KANE. I'm 9, so ... I mean if I were to teach you ...

BELLA. Will you play for me?

A little pause.

Maybe a bit of Dylan? Or, just, / whatever.

KANE. Well I don' 'ave my guitar, so ...

BELLA. One second.

She exits.

He watches her go. Watches the door.

Starts towards his bag –

BELLA enters with a guitar.

He pauses, staring.

Here you are.

KANE. Where'd you ge' tha'?

BELLA. Music room.

She presents it to him, the back facing him.

KANE. Ah, no … No I don' think –

BELLA. Please.

KANE. Nah I don' –

BELLA. Go on, Kane it would be … Don't be embarrassed.

KANE. I'm not. Used to i'. Thing is, I'm …

I'm left-'anded, see, so –

BELLA. I know.

She spins the guitar – it's strung for someone left-handed.

He pauses, staring. She holds it out.

He takes the guitar.

Holds it. Positions it.

Goes to strum –

Stops, looking down at the guitar, shaking his head lightly. Pauses.

She stares.

Can you … not play?

A pause.

Why did you …?

Slight pause.

KANE. I dunno; I …

I dunno.

A pause. He puts the guitar down.

BELLA. Have you told me any other lies?

KANE. No.

BELLA. Any big ones?

KANE. No.

BELLA. Kane.

KANE. No, no other lies.

She gets up close to his face, watching him.

It is clear from his face.

She lets out a noise – part sigh, part cry, part laugh.

BELLA. … no …

She puts her hands to her head; shakes her head.

… no no no, no no no …

He watches her.

I mean … I mean you've got to be …

She pauses.

KANE. Are you … alright, Bella?

Is there … somethin'?

I'm sorry 'bou' the guitar. I's jus' stupid, I jus' like, misspoke 'n' you, you thought I – 'n' I din' wan' t' … dis'ppoint you.

Thought maybe you might like, not wanna, like gi' me tha' ref'rence or …

I mean I'm not lyin'. Bout tha' stuff. I really would. Like to be. A teacher. Y'know? Y'know?

He pauses.

Bella wha's up? I mean maybe tell me? Tell me, we can talk, can't we.

She goes and picks up the baseball bat. Beat.

Yeah I'll / 'ave that back now, thanks. Gonna get rid of i' anyway, so, I'll take tha' …

She goes and stands in front of the door.

Know wha', keep i'. Don' ma'er, anyway, does i', who …

She points the bat at him, stares.

Wha're you doin'? Wha's up?

Bella if you'd actu'lly talk to me … I mean, this is gettin' a li'le … Can we talk 'ere? Can we be calm 'ere?

She wields the bat.

No now le's be calm 'ere; le's not do anythin' we're gonna 'gret 'ere.

/ She walks towards him, the bat raised; he stands his ground.

I 'ssume you ain' gonna do anythin' wi' tha' but if you were, there's people 'round – in the 'ouses – people might –

At a short distance, she raises the bat over her head.

BELLA. … what the fuck.

KANE. Yeah.

BELLA. No what the fuck.

KANE. Yeah no sure.

BELLA. Has anything you've said been –?

KANE. Yeah.

BELLA. Cherry?

KANE. Course she – Wha're you –

BELLA. Is she?

KANE. She passed. I woul'n –

BELLA. Why. Tell me why.

KANE. … why what?

She raises the bat higher.

Yeah, okay, think I ge' wha' yer …

… 'cause …

I dunno …

… jus' 'cause.

BELLA. "Just 'cause"?

KANE. Jus' 'cause.

BELLA. A brain tumour … "just 'cause"?

He pauses. And shrugs.

KANE. In fer a penny.

/ She comes at him, swinging the bat –

BELLA. YOU FUCKER / you fucker you fucker you fucker –

/ He darts away from her around the room.

KANE. … wha' the … wha' the actual …

He gets behind the desk, stops; she's on the other side, she stops too.

BELLA. I know why. I know why.

She flinches one way; he flinches the other.

She flinches the other way; he flinches the first.

She goes for his hand with the bat – he snatches it away just in time – she gets the desk –

KANE. Fuck –

I'm sorry, alright; I'm sorry, yeah? Sorry I bothered you, sorry I've ruined yer night. But ...

So what?

I mean – I'm jus', I'm jus' not dyin'. So ... Tha's good, right? A bit?

Ignore tha', tha' ... one li'le porkie, i's been good. Right? I's been good, Bell.

BELLA. Don't ...

KANE. 'n' I mean ... actu'lly ... really ... di' you actu'lly ... really ... like deep down ...

... do I look sick?

... would I be goin' Japan.

I mean yer a smart lady. To believe all tha' you'd 'ave to be ... gullible as fuck.

She goes over the desk lunging for him; he gets out of the way, just in time.

He flees; she gets between him and the door, and then comes for him.

He climbs up on top of a cupboard, moves to the back; she halts before it.

BELLA. Come down. Come down.

She swings – can't reach him.

She goes to climb up herself; he picks up a box ready to throw it at her.

She weighs it up. Stops.

Know what. Know what, Kane, I think I just wished you were. Dying. And I hope you are. I hope you're really ill, really deeply ill and no one listens.

KANE. Oh, tha's not cool.

A little pause.

You say things like tha' 'n' you wonder why I lied ...

A little pause.

BELLA. Don't you –

Because you're a liar.

KANE. Oh sure.

BELLA. Because / you're a compulsive, bilge-spewing –

KANE. Yeah sure, yeah sure –

BELLA. Who tries to –

KANE. Yeah i's nothin' to do with you, not at all, no.

A little pause.

BELLA. I'm not going anywhere, Kane. You hear me?

A little pause.

KANE. I'll jus' go.

I'll jus' … I'll jus' go, right?

BELLA. No.

KANE. "No"?

Slight pause.

Wha' d'you mean "no"? Wha're you –

You've rumbled me. I'm rumbled. You've got i' out yer system, wi' all the … Now I'll –

BELLA. No.

KANE. "No"?

BELLA. No.

KANE. Stop sayin' "no"; wha're you …?

BELLA. No.

KANE. Christ –

Guess I'll jus' stay up 'ere, then.

Y'know I thought you were a mess lady, but this is some'in' else. Mean you do realise you can' actu'lly kill me, yeah? Can' beat me t'death up 'ere, in yer classroom? So ...

BELLA. I can, hurt you.

KANE. I'm an ex-pupil.

Slight pause.

BELLA. So?

KANE. There not ... rules?

BELLA. No.

KANE. Well you'll've committed, like, assault, right.

BELLA. Self defence.

KANE. No.

He pauses.

Yer the one wi' the bat, I mean ...

He pauses.

You le' me down or I'll go t'yer boss. Tell 'em 'bou' tha' day. The 'ead of tha' new school you wanna go to too. I'll go back t'our old place 'n' talk i' up t'ev'ryone still 'round – 'n' parents, papers – 'n', 'n' yeah, sure – why'd they listen? But I'll still talk. See wha' 'appens. I'll, I'll – day 'n' night – I'll 'aunt you. I don' give a fuck. I got time. I won' stop till ev'ryone knows you 'it a kid – till all 'em think you, you – shoul'n' be allowed – 'in miles of a school – tha' yer fuckin' – meningitis.

Or ... or we can jus' leave i' ... I can go ... 'n' you will never, ever see me again.

A pause.

She comes for him, climbing –

He threatens to throw the box but she's still coming –

He leaps down –

She climbs down and blocks the door, then comes for him –

He flees –

She almost clips his ass –

He gets away and flings things at her –

She's still coming –

He takes up the guitar, and wields it.

She readies the bat and comes for him, ready to fight –

She swings big –

He dodges it and gets round her –

He lunges back, grabs the bat and wrests it from her –

She stumbles, pauses.

Then comes for him with her hands –

He abandons the bat and guitar and grabs her arms –

They struggle, her attempting to hit and kick him –

Her begins to enfold her –

BELLA. Get off me; get –

He is winning –

Get, off, me.

They end up in a bear hug, still for a moment.

She panics; screams:

GET –

He puts his hand over her mouth.

A moment, them standing there.

Then she starts thrashing, screaming under his hand. He struggles to hold her.

It's too much – he lets go; she breaks free and stumbles away, hyperventilating.

… you, you … you, you …

KANE. I'm sorry I –

BELLA. Touch me; you touch me? How, how dare you –

KANE. You were gonna …

He moves towards her slightly.

D'you need a / bag?

BELLA. Stay away from me. Never …

How can you even –?

As if you haven't –

You dirt. You dirt. You shit on my shoe and you –

Ever again I will, I will, I will –

She pauses.

Everyone crying over me hitting you with that thing –
if they'd seen you, if they'd heard what you said – I should've
used it properly. Should've come over and did what everyone
else wanted to – put you down.

A pause. She breathes heavily. He is frozen, staring, eyes wide.

Then his presence changes, and he says:

KANE. "Kane."

She stares at him.

Miss 'ow're you today?

Miss you look lovely.

Miss d'you want some cheese?

Beat.

BELLA. What?

KANE. This's fer you, Miss. We thought we 'an' gi' you a proper welcome to our 'ome, so we got in 'specially some'a the local cheeses.

Now woul' you like Goats, Cranberry, or Inferno t'star'?

He laughs as if he's a class-full of children.

He waits a moment.

"Can you actually just please step outside with me, Kane."

But Miss the cheese'll warm –

"Now."

Wha'e'er you like, Miss. I's yer party.

He pauses for a few seconds.

Is there a problem, Miss.

BELLA. No.

KANE. "Kane, can I –"

BELLA. "In this classroom, Miss?"

Slight pause.

KANE. In this classroom, Miss?

BELLA. "All alone, Miss?"

KANE. All alone, Miss?

"This'll only take a second, Kane."

Is there a problem, Miss.

"Yes, Kane."

BELLA. "Yes there is actually, Kane."

KANE. "Yes there is actually, Kane."

"Kane, can I ask why you –"

BELLA. Why you brought a cheese board into school?

Slight pause. Her hair is different now.

KANE. I's my lunch, Miss. My Mum gave it me.

BELLA. I don't think that's true, Kane, though I could call your mother to find out?

KANE. Sure.

BELLA. We're going to go back in and you're going to gather up that cheese, and go see Mr Webber with it. I think he'll be able to guess why I've sent you.

KANE. Okay Miss.

BELLA. And no actually, Kane. Listen to me, please. I am absolutely sick to death of you interrupting my lessons.

KANE. I've got ADHD.

BELLA. Sure, / but –

KANE. "I don't care."

Little pause.

BELLA. What?

KANE. Not "sure" – "I don't care."

Little pause.

BELLA. No.

You put off the other kids, you insult me, and frankly you're just doing yourself harm. If you keep interrupting my lessons, I will have to ask for you to be removed.

KANE. "Remove you."

BELLA. Go get your stuff.

KANE. "Remove" –

BELLA. GO AND get your ...

KANE. ... alright, Miss ...

KANE starts having his physical reaction to the words. Slight at first, it grows stronger and stronger; a vibration, building.

I jus' don' unnerstan' why I'm the one who's always –

BELLA. We're near the desk?

KANE. Yeah –

picked on, called out, made to leave 'n' – 'n' – 'n' – 'n' –

Miss you said –

BELLA. You said –

KANE. No you said –

BELLA. No you said – You turned around and you said –

KANE. "Fucking chav families ..."

A pause. She stares at him.

You mu'ered it. On yer way out.

BELLA. ... no I didn't.

KANE. Yes you did; unner yer breath.

BELLA. No I ... I'm sure you turned around and you, you started off on ...

KANE. I di'n't, Miss.

BELLA. I ... I wouldn't ... I –

KANE. Say it. Please.

A pause.

Say it.

BELLA. … fucking chav families …

KANE has a nosebleed now. He smears it across his cheek, shaking.

KANE. Bitch.

BELLA. I'm sorry?

KANE. Yer a fuckin' bitch.

BELLA. Kane.

KANE. We 'ate you. We all do. Ev'ryone.

BELLA. That's enough, go see –

KANE. Yer 'sgustin'. Yer 'air, yer big fangs, yer awful skin. We all think yer 'sgustin'.

His physical reaction is growing still.

You, you – You should –

BELLA. "Sand nigger."

KANE. Sand nigger.

BELLA. Kane –

"You are, we all say you are. Yer a sand nigger."

That's –

He gets up in her face; he's thrumming, she can hear it.

HELLO? SOMEONE? CAN SOMEONE COME IN HERE AND HELP –?

"Rag-'ead."

KANE. Rag-'ead, you've got a –

BELLA. "Paki-slut"; "camel-fucker" –

You …

KANE. Darky whore; arab cunt –

BELLA. You're scum.

KANE. Firecracker; glass nigger –

BELLA. Dirt on my shoe.

KANE. Cairo coon; clitless fucking –

BELLA. You should be sterilised, wiped out –

KANE. You think you jus' come 'ere? Come 'ere, be 'owever you want?

Actin' like yer one of us, when, when, when yer –

You know. You know. Why you do it; why you 'urt me.

Plannin', laughin' 'ind yer 'and front'a class –

We'll murder you. Yeah? Murder, you.

Stab you; burn you; rape –

My dad says, knock you down in street –

I say pick up nearest metal 'n', 'n', 'n' –

You deserve i'. No one'll 'elp you.

We're waitin'.

You watch.

One day –

one day –

one –

He grabs her hand and forces it onto the penholder; she pulls her arm away –

BELLA. No. Stop. Kane. It's done. Stop. I said –

He lets go of her arm; slaps her face.

YOU –

She grabs his face with her left hand; he bites the webbing, hard —

She screams and grabs the penholder with her right; raises it high —

He closes his eyes; puts his chin to his chest —

And she brings the edge down on his crown, hard.

He grunts, sways.

She pauses for a moment; raises it again, higher.

And halts, looking at him, bowed. His head is bleeding.

She's frozen.

Then she spins and smashes the metal down on onto the desk again and again and again and —

He sits down, swaying.

again and she drops the metal —

spins and spits on his head —

wobbles on her feet —

walks away, shaking.

She looks at her hands: they're bleeding. She gets tissues, wipes her hands, casts the tissues away.

Well. D'you feel any better now?

No? No?

She gets her cover letter, and his lighter. Holds the letter over the bin, before him. Sets the letter alight, staring at him.

He doesn't look up.

She drops the burning letter into the bin.

Right.

She pauses.

She goes and gets his vodka, and sits away from him.

She drinks it.

She pauses. She holds the bottle out to him. A pause.

He comes over to her, takes the bottle, and sits. He drinks.

She gets some cigarettes from her bag. Lights one. Has a drag.

He has a big glug; coughs.

Yeah. Makes my heart burn.

He motions for the cigarette; she holds it out; they swap bottle and cigarette.

They share the spirit and the cigarettes, until they're ready to speak again.